Johann David Michaelis

A Dissertation on the Influence of Opinions on Language and

of Language on Opinions

Johann David Michaelis

A Dissertation on the Influence of Opinions on Language and of Language on Opinions

ISBN/EAN: 9783337157821

Printed in Europe, USA, Canada, Australia, Japan

Cover: Foto ©ninafisch / pixelio.de

More available books at **www.hansebooks.com**

A

DISSERTATION

ON THE

INFLUENCE OF OPINIONS ON LANGUAGE

AND OF

LANGUAGE ON OPINIONS,

WHICH GAINED THE

PRUSSIAN Royal Academy's Prize on that Subject.

CONTAINING

Many Curious Particulars in Philology, Natural History, and the Scriptural Phraseology.

TOGETHER WITH

AN ENQUIRY

INTO THE

Advantages and Practicability of an UNIVERSAL LEARNED LANGUAGE.

By Mr. MICHAELIS,

Court-Counsellor to His BRITANNIC Majesty, and Director of the Royal Society at GOTTINGEN.

THE SECOND EDITION.

LONDON,

Printed for W. OWEN, in Fleet-Street; J. JOHNSON, in St. Paul's Church-Yard; and W. BINGLEY, in Newgate-Street.
MDCCLXXI.
[Price Five Shillings.]

Heads of Colleges, Masters of Academies, and other Seminaries of Learning:

GENTLEMEN,

THE propriety of dedicating this piece to you, as the best judges of its contents, and whose more immediate province it is to remove such mistakes and abuses intimated therein as subsist among us, will excuse the liberty of this dedication.

Wishing the most desirable success to your endeavours, as very nearly connected with the improvement of the human mind, and the public good, I remain with great respect,

GENTLEMEN,

Your most humble Servant,

THE TRANSLATOR.

THE
PREFACE.

THE discourse, of which the following sheets are a translation, was crowned by the Royal Academy of Berlin in 1759, and we flatter ourselves that it will be the more acceptable to the public, as in the collection of the pieces which concurred for the prize, this, contrary to custom, has appeared only in the German tongue. But what chiefly determined us is, on one hand, the importance of the subject, as concerning philosophers of all times and all nations; and on the other, that masterly strength with which this subject is here handled by one of the most celebrated scholars in Germany; so that, with all the inferiority of a translation, and from so great an original, we hope the good office herein intended to foreigners, will meet with a kind acceptance.

Judicious readers, in a work of this kind, seek fruits more than blossoms; accordingly the translator endeavoured only

only to be clear and exact. M. *Michaëlis* himself has condescended to revise a manuscript of the translation; and what gives this edition a great advantage over the German is, his having enriched it with very considerable supplements; among which the Literati will with pleasure see an excellent dissertation on the project of an universal language*.

* The authors of the *Bibliotheque des Beaux Arts*, in their account of Mr. *Michaëlis*'s Dissertation, give the following short history of this scheme, which has so exercised some philosophic geniuses.

We first find that *Descartes*, being consulted by father *Mersenne* concerning the plan of an universal language, of which an anonymous Frenchman had given a sketch, that great philosopher indeed disapproved its extent: it appeared to him in some respects chimerical; but, on the other hand, he allowed of the possibility of the thing itself; and, what is more, took the trouble of committing to paper what he thought of it, and the best method for executing it. *Cartes epist.* part i. epist. iii. That method *Kircher* afterwards endeavoured to carry into execution, in a book published by him at Rome, 1665, under the title of Ars *Polygraphica*, fol. See Morhof. *Polyhist.* lib. iv. cap. ii. tom. i. p. 729. but with that little success, which *Descartes* had prognosticated to the French author: *Existimo possibilem esse hanc linguam, & reperiri posse scientiam eam ex qua illa pendet, cujus certe beneficio rusticus quispiam de rerum veritate posset melius judicare quam jam philosophus aliquis. Sed ne' speres te unquam visurum illam in usum, & tam magnas in orbe mutationes supponit, essetque necesse totum orbem in terrestrem paradisum converti; quod sane in fabulis tantum locum habeat.* Cartes, ibid.

Before *Kircher*, and perhaps before any others we shall speak of, *Beccherus* had undertaken to form a characteristic, and published his plan at Francfort in 1661, with this title, *Character pro Notitia Linguarum Universalis*, &c. and of which a new edition appears to have come out at the same place in 1668.

A native of Scotland, who kept a private grammar-school at Oxford, had also written on the same subject in the year 1661 : his name was *George Dalgarno*, or *Dalgarne :* he printed at London, in octavo, *Ars signorum, vulgo character universalis & lingua philosophica, qua poterunt homines diversissimorum idiomatum spatio duarum septimanarum omnia animi sui sensa, non minus intelligibiliter, sive scribendo, sive loquendo, mutuo communicare quam linguis propriis vernaculis*, &c. This work was, by the learned, judged to abound with erudition and pedantry.

Wood imagined that *Dalgerno* had communicated the manuscript of it to Dr. *Wilkins*, afterwards bishop of Chester, and that from it, the bishop conceived his first idea of that arduous subject, on which in 1668 he published his famous book, entitled *An essay towards a real character, and a philosophical language* (a) : an extract of which book is to be found in the philosophical transactions, No. 35. But as the learned authors of the new *Dictionaire historique & critique*, have very well observed on *Art. Wilkins*. It is evident from another book of the bishops, which he published at London 1641, with the title of *Mercury, or the secret and speedy messenger: shewing a safe and speedy manner of communicating one's thoughts to a distant friend*. It is, we say, incontestable, that this learned person had meditated and drawn the plan of an universal character, at least twenty years before *Delgarno*'s book saw the light. Dr. *Wilkins*'s book was received with great applause by some of the learned : Mr. *Hook*, among others, recommended it as the best plan that could be conceived.

(a) Wood, *Athen. Oxon.* vol. ii. col. 5, 7.

But

But we learn from M. *Fontenelle*'s fine eulogium on *Leibnitz*. *Hist. de l' Acad. des Sci.* 1716. pag. 148. edit. Amst. that this great man was of another opinion. According to him, neither *Wilkins* nor *Delgarno* had hit on the true *real characters*, which he esteemed the noblest instrument ever offered to the human mind, and which, said he, must exceedingly facilitate both reasoning, memory, and invention.

Leibnitz was unalterably persuaded, that these characters must be like those made use of in algebra. He said, that he was busied about *an alphabet of human thoughts*, as introductory to a philosophic language; but death prevented his carrying that project into full execution. However, among the papers of that great man, were found a Latin treatise on that subject, and several pieces relating to it; which a learned Hanoverian gives us to hope will be published.

M. *Fontenelle* did not hold this scheme to be in any wise chimerical: " The " difficulty, said he, is not to invent the most simple, the most easy, and the " most convenient characters; but to prevail with the several nations to make " use of them. Unfortunately, they agree in nothing but in not being sensible " of their common interests."

We must wait for what M. de *Premontval* will offer to the public on this head. The repetition of schemes, may perhaps bring to light a characteristic of easier execution, than any which have hitherto been proposed: till then, M. *Michaëlis*'s arguments must hold good.

THE

THE

INTRODUCTION.

I Take the liberty to divide the academy's problem; as to me seems most proper for unfolding and solving it.

I shall first speak to the influence of the opinions of a people on the language; and the academy itself having judged this part of the question to be the more easy, I shall only support an incontestable proposition, with some instances which serve for its farther illustration. This proposition will likewise receive an additional light from observations; which, to avoid repetitions, I refer to the following sections. In the second part, I shall treat of the beneficial influences; and in the third, of the noxious influences of some languages on opinions and sciences. Lastly, I shall canvass the means of preventing one, and promoting the other.

ERRATA.

Page 1. l. 4. for from origin *read* from its origin. p. 4. l. 27 for and *r*. him. p. 12. l. 1. dele to. p. 13. note *s*. for febrigue *r*. febrifuge. p. 15. l. 3. for habits *r*. habit. p. 19. l. 11. for loaded *r*. load. p. 21. l. 4. for so *r*. to. p. 22. l. 23. for imposts *r*. imparts. p. 25. l. 31. dele so. p. 32. l. 13. dele for. p. 37. l. 17. for younger *r*. early. p. 41. l. 11. *r*. omniscience too. p. 44. l. 7. for naturalists *r*. naturalis. p. 46. note *t*. l. 1. for having *r*. has. p. 47 l. 14. for lesser *r*. less. p. 49. l. 11. for homon; my *r*. homonimy. p. 49. l. 14. for unexcepted *r*. unexpected. p. 51. l. 2. for certain, *r*. certainly. p. 51. l. 3. for it is *r*. is it. p. 52. l. 2. for comatentiona, *r*. collection. p. 56. note *k*. for celo, *r*. cielo. p. 68. l. 7. for bear *r*. bears. p. 73. l. 11. *r*. language. p. 75. l. 4. for influence *r*. influences.

A DISSERTATION

ON THE

Influence of Opinions, &c.

SECTION I.

The influence of a people's opinions on the languages.

ALL objects prefent themfelves to our mind under a certain appearance, and by this appearance it is, that the names we give them and our defcriptions of them are ever regulated. Nothing is more evident; fuppofe that every people had from origin been accuftomed to a particular fyftem of botany; undoubtedly, the vegetables comprehended, among thefe different people, under the fame generical appellation would not be the fame. Though, there be not, between languages, a diftinction fo learned and fo fyftematical; ftill this fiction reprefents to us at large and more manifeftly, what muft happen in various particulars, among nations of a different way of thinking. There is no language, the origin of which is not, by many centuries, prior to that of the fyftems of botany which we are now acquainted with; likewife there are none in which may not be obferved traces of the infancy of botany, of that rude and uncultivated knowledge of vegetables, which was the utmoft attainment of the early ages: befides thofe of a vifible refemblance,

they

they often comprehended under the same denomination those which were employed for the like uses, whatever might be their other differences. This method was likewise that of the most antient professed botanists; they divided the classes of plants according to the respective benefits reaped from them. All this was no more than natural. The first motive for human attention fixing itself on the products of nature is their use, this is the character which, as it most concerns us, strikes us previously and beyond all others.

All opinions are not received into the language; in that, neither the scholars authority nor his demonstrations are regarded, however intimately he himself may be convinced of the truth of his doctrines. He may make a clamour about the justness of expressions, he may protest against vulgar errors; no body minds him. In short, language is a democracy where use or custom is decided by the majority; and Horace has pronounced that in languages custom is the supreme law. For instance, should a stickler for Copernicus and the true system of the world, carry his zeal so far as to say *the city of Berlin sets at such and such an hour*, instead of making use of the common expression, *the sun sets at Berlin at such an hour*, he speaks the truth to be sure; but his manner of speaking it is pedantry. There is only one particular wherein the empire of language seems to differ from democracy; that often the commonalty take their rule of speech from persons of education, but is not the like seen in all democratical states? Is it not a frequent case for a citizen conscious of his ignorance gladly to defer to the opinion of one whom he conceives to have more knowledge and understanding? We need not therefore depart from a comparison which so well represents, what it is intended to represent.

It is from the opinions of the people and the point of view, in which objects appear to them, that language receives its form. As literature and politeness gain ground in a nation, and according to the duration of their reign, they extend their influences in the language, the commonality in such times, acquiring the knowledge of several expressions invented by the learned, as on the other hand, the latter not seldom adopt popular expressions. If it be considered that Greece, and especially the city of Athens, were eminently possessed of this advantage, the great prerogatives of the Greek

language

language will no longer be wondered at. To this influence philofophy and the feveral branches of literature principally contribute, efpecially when from the duft of the ftudy, they pafs into the mouths both of the profane and facred orator, or thofe pretty mouths, which the graces feem to animate, and whofe every word meets with ecchos, delighting to repeat it. How many new words has not the Wolfian philofophy introduced into our language, and how many words has it not ftripped of their former import? But all this is nothing in comparifon of the confequences, when poets of celebrity carry philofophy to the fummit of Parnaffus, and embellifh it with the charms of the mufes. Being efteemed claffical authors, every body is eager to read them, all their innovations are acquiefced to, their very faults, in company with fo many beauties, are admired, and have their imitators. Now, only let a knot of perfons of wit make ufe of thefe new expreffions as approving them, this alone brings them into repute; the very commonality affect them; they fpread into univerfal vogue.

Not that I pretend to deny, but that one fingle man, and who, far from a claffical author, is, as I may fay, only a private individual in the empire of language, may happen to ftrike out an expreffion which, with the ideas relative to it, fhall be admitted into a language. For inftance, a witty faying comes from one, it pleafes the hearers, it is thought juft and pretty, or fine, or ftrong, many repeat it, it even meets with plagiaries who father it, thus it runs from mouth to mouth, till it grows into a kind of proverb. Thus it is that thoufands of men become contributors to that immenfe heap of truths and errors, of which the languages of nations are the repofitories; but what every particular individual furnifhes is little or nothing: moft hazarded expreffions do not take; they are like bloffoms of which the greater part drop from the trees and come to nothing: and even if a new term does take, it does not neceffarily follow that it annihilates the former: the language, poffibly, retains both. The right of creating as we have faid before, properly belongs only to claffic authors, the fair fex, and the people, who are indeed the fupreme legiflators.

Thefe are the propofitions, which I am now to prove by inftances.

The Greek name of the deity (*a*) is derived from a verb, which signifies, *to run, to move one's self*, and many hold that this name was originally appropriated to the stars, as the deities which were worshipped at the time of the formation of the language, and from thence their name came to be that of the deity.

Reason, in explaining the origin of the world, requires only one God, but superstition has strangely multiplied the number, and this has affected the languages, particularly in the Latin, it has left very strongly marked traces. The Latin word for God may be said to be only plural; as for *Deus* in the singular number, its meaning does not correspond with the word *Dieu* in French, or *Gott* in German. Whenever we hear these words, we immediately think on the only one God, and we make use of them as a proper name, without any article; whereas the *Deus* of the Latins denotes one God amongst several, and should be rendered in French *le Dieu, the God*, when this God is characterized by what goes before; and when not, *un des Dieux, one of the Gods*, or simply, *un Dieu, a God*. This admits of some exceptions, but I speak of what is most usual.

It may even be said that the Greeks, no less than the Latins, are without a term to express the idea which we form to ourselves of God, I mean that of a supreme, independant, infinitely perfect Being, who has created the world. The Gods of the Romans, and the Demons of the Greeks, were only spirits superior to man by their power and the excellence of their nature; they were nothing more than those whom the church has stiled angels (*b*), their origin was quite as contingent, and their essence not less limited; like them they were only ministers and vicars of the true God. Of this God some philosophers seemed to have had a remote view, and to have discerned and as it were through a veil; their most laboured definitions of him were extremely vague, inadequate and imperfect. What if they sometimes give him the epithets of *sovereign*, of *master of the Gods*, of *supreme God*, what if they call him *the thunder hurling God*, the *God who drives his thundering car along the clouds*, &c. These descriptions

---

(*a*) Θεός.
(*b*) Of what the English call *Superior beings*.

were

were very far from being in their language so determinate, as the word denoting the Deity is in ours; they might indeed imply the notion of an intelligence of the first order, but finite and dependent. So that these languages had, in reality, the fault attributed to the Chinese, and it is with less reason that the latter is said to have no name for the Deity, as having no other than that of *Sky*. It is to the Christian religion that we are beholden for a word which expresses, without any confusion or ambiguity, the philosophical idea of an infinite substance, Creator of the universe, and which distinguishes that substance from all intermediate spirits and angels, even in churches, where those spirits have a worship of adoration paid to them.

The opinions of the Jews produced in the Greek language, which was spoken at Alexandria, and elsewhere among that nation, a quite contrary effect. The Greeks often gave to their Gods the names of *Demon* and *Demonion*, and these Gods the Jews took to be angels; but imagining the pagan deities to be sensitive and taking delight in the worship paid to them, they necessarily could take them only for rebel angels and such as were fallen from their exalted origin. And that this was the real idea they entertained of such spirits is well known, and farther that they had transmitted it not only to the Christians but even the Arabs: in a word, the most manifest impress of it appears in their language: in the Greek of the Jews, I mean the Greek bible, the word *demonion* signifies a devil.

Every language, before it has gone through philosophic hands, must of necessity be wanting in proper terms for denoting such objects which do not come within the verge of the senses, and especially metaphisical ideas. Thus Ludolph informs us, that the Ethiopians, having but one word for *nature* and *person*, could not distinguish those two things in the controversy concerning Christ's two natures.

On the other hand, when a language has followed philosophy through its several revolutions, there will be some change in the meaning and import of its philosophic terms. To most Germans the word *essence* or being (c), carries with it an idea agreeable to the Wolfian definition, an idea

(c) Wesen.

however,

however, very different from that which divines annexed to it, long before Leibnitz was so much as born, when they said *that the essence of God is one.* I make no doubt that many still give a modern sense to that proposition, as couched in our old language; and then they certainly will find nothing mysterious in the doctrine of the trinity. They will conceive the divine essence common to three persons just as easily as they conceive the human essence common to millions of persons. Formerly *essence* signified what at present is meant by *existence* or *reality*, and Luther, without the least ambiguity might render the 11th verse of the 4th chapter of the Revelations, *Durch deinen Willen haben sie das* Wesen, i. e. of thy will they hold their essence; but philosophy having introduced some change into the language, this passage became obscure, that a commentary was wanting to it, and one of our divines, Mr. Reinbeck, who had the courage to explain Luther in a rational manner, met with an adversary, who denied the eternity of philosophic essences, maintaining that those very essences were produced by God and depended on his will.

 The name by which the Germans call the leprosy is taken from the external figure as it appears to our eyes *(d)*. All over the East, where this distemper is almost incurable it was looked on as a punishment of God's own immediate inflicting. From holy scripture we know that this was the opinion of the Jews, and according to Herodotus, it was the belief of the Persians, that the leprosy came no other way than as a punishment for having offended the sun. From hence it is that the most usual word for the leprosy, among the Hebrews, properly signifies *a stroke or lash with a whip (e).*

 (d) The German name for the leprosy is auffatz or excrescence, which may signify the formation of scales on the skin.

 (e) In Arabic, صرب (Tsari) *is a whip or scourge,* and صرع (Tsaraa) *to whip or scourge.* The passage of Herodotus is as follows. If any of the citizens have a leprosy or scrofulous disease he is not permitted to stay within the city, nor to converse with other persons; having as they believed drawn this punishment upon himself by committing some offence against the sun, and if strangers are infected with those distempers they are immediately expelled the country, and, from motives of the same kind, white pigeons are not suffered to be kept.

The

[7]

The Greek word for a *soul* likewise signifies a butterfly *(f)*. The Greeks had observed the metamorphosis which the catterpiller goes through, and several among them, who believed the immortality of souls, imagined that, at death, they only quitted their nympha to be invested with a divine nature. For this reason it was that they made the butterfly the hieroglyphic for representing the soul, and at length conferred on that insect the very name of the soul.

The Babylonians had a notion, that a grub *(g)* or kind of wasp went from the fruit of the male palm-tree into the date of the female palm-tree, and impregnated it *(h)*. Whatever may have been in this opinion, it had an influence on the Arabian language, between which and the Chaldean spoken at Babylon, there was only a dialectical difference. The Arabians denoted the blossom of the male palm-tree *(i)* by a name which, literally translated, signifies the *palm-tree flies (k)*; and the Persians, to describe the fecundation of the female palm-tree by the male palm-tree, make use of the expression *to apply the flies (l)*.

Here is another very remarkable passage, but the placing it in its full light indispensibly leads me into a grammatical subtilty. The Orientals, by whom I mean those several people whose languages were derived from one common source, as the Arabs, the Syrians, the Chaldeans, and the Hebrews: the Orientals, I say, seem, from time immemorial, to have been acquainted with the sexes of plants, which, in our northern coun-

---

(f) Ψυχή

(g) Ψήν. Vermiculus in caprificis nascens.

(h) The palm-tree grows naturally all over the plain of Babylon, and the greater part bear fruit, of which they make bread, wine, and honey. This tree is cultivated as the fig-tree, tying the fruit of that which the Grecians call the male palm about these trees which bear dates, to the end that a gnat may enter and ripen the fruit; for the fruit of the male palm, like that of the wild fig-tree, produces a gnat. Herodotus, l. 1.

(i) Spatha masculina.

(k) Anbaar Elnachi. v. Kæmpferi Amœnitates exot 8. p. 696.

(l) Ambaar dadan. ib. p. 708. it must be noticed that Kæmpfer, being unacquainted with that opinion, translates this otherwise; but though his meaning of the word *Ambder* be used in the Persian language, it is not in the Arabic.

C tries,

tries, is a discovery of no later date than the present age; and this is not to be wondered at, they had every where before them the palm-tree, in which the two sexes are manifest beyond dispute: and it was just as natural to conclude from that tree to other vegetables, as to conclude from animals in whom the difference of sex is visible, to those in whom it is, as it were latent. The more the male palm-tree resembles the female palm-tree before the fruit ripens, the stronger must the presumption have been of a difference of sexes in those vegetables where the organs of generation are not obvious to the sight; but the mind of man which delights in analogies, and is for casting all nature in the same mould, refines on every thing, and spoils truths by overstraining them. The Orientals thought every thing had its duplicate. *God*, says Mahomet, *has created nothing which is not male and female: this holds good in all the productions of the earth, it holds good of souls, and even of things where you little apprehend any such thing (m)*. With such a turn of mind, may not they have imagined those parts of our bodies, of which we have two, to be male and female, and this opinion actually occurs in the Arabic, Syriac, and Hebrew languages; and these languages may be said equally to favour both sexes. To the double members they give a masculine termination and a feminine construction *(n)*; and in a passage of the second book of Chronicles, where mention is made of the cherubs two wings, the construction even alternates, being masculine for the right wing and feminine for the left *(o)*.

On considering that the Hebrews use a similar licence relatively to the names of animals, and that often, without the least regard to the ani-

(*m*) Chap. **XXXVI**.

(*n*) For this I refer the reader to Espenius's Arabic grammar, p. 135, to the Syriac grammar of M. Michaelis, professor at Hull, p. 30; and the Hebrew grammar, by M. Michaelis, professor at Gottingen, p. 226, is a farther proof of this peculiarity.

(*o*) 2 Chronicles iii. 11. The following translation in barbarous Latin may clear up this to those who are unacquainted with the Hebrew.

Et ala *cherubi alterius* exporrectus *erat* ad *parietem* templi et ala altera conjuncta *alæ cherubi prioris*

mal's

mal's fex, they conftrue as feminine words of a mafculine termination; and that this mode of conftruction is particular to this clafs of nouns and relative to the double fex of animals, their affecting for the double members a fingularity fo very remote from the genius of other languages, will be the lefs queftioned.

There is a kind of calcareous earth, refembling meal, of which inventive hunger has often made ufe in times of dearth; and by feveral it has even been accounted real meal, and a donation of heavenly bounty for the relief of the indigent: and this miftake has procured it in the German language a name which may be rendered *mountain-meal (p)*. This name is univerfally ufed, and the learned themfelves, to be underftood, are obliged to conform to it; thus it will in its turn be a means of perpetuating the miftake from whence it took its rife, a miftake by which thoufands perhaps have fuffered, and will fuffer. But this laft confideration belongs to my third fection.

(p) Bergmehl. M. Gefner who did me the honour of reading over this piece after the firft edition of it at Berlin, informs me of an objection which feems well grounded. Inftead of the miftake giving rife to the name, he rather thinks that the name occafions the fatal miftake. Whatever is like meal, whatever feems to have been pulverifed may in the German language be called *mehl* meal, as in fome parts of Germany wood reduced to duft by worms is called worm-mehl. This opinion of Mr. Gefner's is farther countenanced by etymology: *mehl* meal being derived from *mahlen* to grind, confequently this inftance belongs to the third fection.

Concerning this production, Mr. Da Cofta in his hiftory of foffils has the following particulars: in England we are not deftitute of this earth, the quarries of Oxfordfhire afford it, and Dr. Woodward received it from the late quarries at Colly Wefton in Northamptonfhire. It is very frequently found in the fiffures of ftone in the quarries about Sherbourne, in Gloucefterfhire, loofe along with the fpare. I have likewife found it greatly mixed with fpar in the coal pits of Leicefterfhire and Derbyfhire. Its medical ufes are many.

In Malta it abounds and the inhabitants make it into fmall cakes, which they ftamp with the figures of faints, efpecially of St. Paul, indeed they generally call it *gratia di St. Paulo*.

SECTION.

SECTION II.

Of the advantageous influence of languages on opinions.

THE proofs of the advantageous influence of language on opinions I reduce to a few classes, the number of which unquestionably might be greatly augmented, but I shall not so much as go about an enumeration of them; the subject I well know is inexhaustible.

I. There are happy etymologies, they comprehend accurate descriptions, real definitions, which clear the meanings and disperse that kind of mist in which they are so often involved. These etymologies, besides preventing many errors and altercations about words, make known to him whose happiness it is to meet with such in his language, I say they immediately make known to him truths of which, philosophers, less favoured by their language, purchase the attainment by laborious study.

When we either pronounce or hear the word *glory*, we all think something, and in some measure the same thing. We understand the word, but as to its etymology we are totally in the dark, it conveys no more instruction to us than if we had made use of an Algebraic character, for instance expressing glory by Z. This word does not make known to us in what glory consists, it rectifies no error, it does not undeceive either the hare-brained hero, infatuated with the phantom of glory, nor the saturnine moralist who affects a contempt of it. The very philosopher, misled by an arbitrary sound which custom has annexed to so many confused ideas, and often to very false ideas, will give us false definitions. This has been the case more than once. *Glory* has been confounded with the cause productive of it, I mean with internal perfection; it has been defined *the sum of all our perfections*, and, in conformity to that notion, we have been taught that the glory of God does not depend on his creatures, nor the glory of the wise man on what others think of him. These doctrines which, in the main, turn only on an ambiguity, are with many become so sacred and respectable that their zeal would be extremely offended against any who should take it into their heads to contest them. If this definition, however, be just, either the philosopher from whom we received it, or our language must be without a word for expressing the favourable opinion the world entertains of our good actions.

The Greek language has a great advantage in this point. The word Δοξα, which signifies glory, is, at the same time, a real definition of it, and a definition pregnant with consequences. This word properly means *opinion*, and is made use of to denote *glory*, as consisting in the good opinion the world has of us (*q*). Εν δοξη ειναι *is to be in the good opinion of others* (*r*), and δοκιμος, is one of whom the public has a good opinion.

Thus, the Greeks could not but know in what glory consists; this etymology was continually putting them in mind of it; and to imagine that there could be any such thing as glory independantly of the high opinion entertained of our talents and virtues, they must have forgotten their very mother-tongue. As for the metaphysician, it was scarce possible for him to deviate from the common mode of thinking, so far as to pretend, that God enjoys glory amidst the solitude of eternity; and if an affectation of paradox, or a want of attending to the language, had carried him to that absurdity, there was no Greek so void of sense as not to see that God's perfections could not be acknowledged or celebrated whilst God alone existed.

This idea of glory which the Greek expression conveyed, farther shewed, that it was not to be attained by guilt, violence, and devastation; but by virtues, by generosity and benevolence; this, in consequence, made glory to be a real good; for, if we consider how much our prosperity or adversity, our happiness or unhappiness, depend on others, their good or bad opinion certainly will not be a matter of indifference to us; and that misanthropical doctor, who represents glory to us as an airy vapour, as a

---

(*q*) See a work of M. Gesner's, intituled *Aristotelea de Gloria*.

(*r*) Σπαρτιητεων δοκιμος, *one regarded among the Spartans* or of whom all the Spartans had a good opinion, as Lycurgus is called in Herodotus, l. 1. Δοκιμος τοις ανθρωποις. Romans xiv. 18. who has a good character, and is esteemed among men.

chimera,

chymera, teaches a doctrine not less diffonant from human nature, and to the situation we are placed in here below, than as if he was to exhort us to be independant like the Deity, and, like him, to stand in no need of the assistance and good offices of another. In this view the desire of glory, that desire so vilified, becomes a commendable disposition, tending to make of all mankind a society of brethren, prompting every one to seek the approbation of his fellow creatures, and to acquire it by a decent and virtuous behaviour.

To give a clear notion of glory to the sour bigot, who professes the most supercilious contempt of it is, I own, no easy matter; and were it possible to bring him to better thoughts, it would be effected in Greek sooner than in any other language. You are are obliged, would I say to him, to seek that glory which consists in a good reputation: the most natural punishment annexed to bad actions is the loss of honour: to make light of this, is shaking off the only curb which, humanly speaking, can keep you to your duty: you will gradually become a profligate, hardened in guilt, and then to be dealt with only by bodily punishment.

It cannot be imagined how much good is contained in etymology. It is a treasure of sense, knowledge, and wisdom: it includes truths which most philosophers do not see into, and will one day immortalize the philosopher who shall discover them, without so much as having himself apprehended, that, from time immemorial, they have been in every body's mouth. This is not at all strange. Languages are an accumulation of the wisdom and genius of nations, and to which every one has contributed something: let not this be understood of the learned only, who, on the contrary, have often but a narrow genius, who are still more often blinded by prepossession, and who, after all, scarce make the hundredth part of mankind. The bare man of wit perhaps is a larger contributor, and the illiterate has often a greater share in it, his thoughts being, as I may say, more nearly allied to nature. The heretic shall sometimes contribute to it what the orthodox preacher will carefully avoid, the former thinking more freely, and his point of view being less confined. It is likewise not seldom seen that even the orthodox, the most exasperated against heresies, shall yet adopt their language, if they are but strangers to the mint where

where it was coined. The genius even of children, when in their first vigour, and void of all prejudices, shall produce happy strokes, bold associations of ideas, yet evidently true, all increasing and enriching this national treasure. Cheerfulness, which utters truths unknowingly, sprightly company, wine which expands the genius, poetry which, in its enthusiasm, brings forth so many novelties, medlies of truth and fiction, are all so many sources conveying into the languages their peculiar expressions. Suppose this to have gone on twenty or forty centuries; during this space of time many truths, at first admitted and afterwards rejected, as likewise many truths never taken notice of as such, and looked only as mere witticisms, have, however, met with an expression or phrase in which they have been retained, and thus perpetually incorporated with the language. Should the virtue of Quinquina, (the Jesuits bark) through the negligence of the physicians, or the return of universal barbarism, come to be mistaken or forgotten in Germany, with only the bare name remaining, the bare name would sufficiently inform our posterity of the use of Quinquina among us (*s*): so that language is a kind of archives, where the discoveries of men are safe from any accidents, archives which are proof against fire, and which cannot be destroyed but with the total ruin of the people.

Grammarians often bestow very great encomiums on etymology. That it never proves the truth of a proposition I allow; but it preserves truths; it is a kind of library, containing a great number of useful discoveries. It includes in one word as much good philosophy as any system whatever. I farther allow, that this fountain of truths may become a fountain of errors, when the grammarian or philosopher are for drawing from it proof of their assertions or real definitions, its stream is not perfectly pure, truths and errors float in it confusedly intermixed.

Etymological propositions I think may be compared to those loose detached propositions, of which collections are published under the title of *Thoughts*, without adducing any kind of proof. What I perceive in every etymology is, that, in such, or such a nation, some body has thought

(*s*) Quinquina is in German called *Fieberrinde*, i. e. fever-bark, or the febrigue-bark or rind.

thus

thus or thus; but to know whether his thoughts be right or wrong requires a particular inquiry, which has nothing to do with etymology. Here again it will bear a comparison with libraries, the good and the bad being intermixed in them. A sensible man will never subscribe to a phylosophical thesis only from having seen it in black and white in some corner of a library; neither will he explode the use of libraries purely because old books contain a great many falsities, or because the truths to be met with in them are not accompanied with their proofs: some, on the contrary, will be the better pleased with this omission of the proofs, as leaving to the reflective reader the honour and satisfaction of finding them out.

The learned, the reformers of sciences, the discoverers of new truths' etymology furnishes with the means of spreading and perpetuating their discoveries. They will be preserved much more securely in a name adapted to the genius of the language than in perishable books, the fashion of which passeth away, that after a certain time, they are no longer read. But the grand secret is to bring this name into vogue; the coining of it is easy, but not so the making it current; in this only classic authors can succeed, and especially poets, to whom this honour seems peculiarly reserved. That extreme care and delicacy with which the antients applied themselves to purify and embelish their language, was so very far from being a ridiculous pedantry, that our literati should imitate their application. How is the merit of poetry inhanced in the mouth of a great genius? a merit abundantly rewarding those hours which his commerce with the muses has deprived him of. Suppose the illustrious Mr. Haller, who, to the most extensive knowledge of botany, joins the most elevated spirit of poetry, and who, both in prose and verse, is one of the finest writers in all Germany. Suppose, I say, he were, both in his poems and other writings, to distinguish by particular names those parts of the vegetables which characterise their sex, calling them, for instance, *the male and the female*, these appellations once received, would not only immortalize in Germany one of the finest modern discoveries, but would render this discovery intelligible to every one. Now what a service would this be to the nation and to truth?

There

There is another cause of this great fecundity of etymologies: several objects have undergone so many changes, that it is extremely difficult to know them again distinctly; and habits familiarizing us with them from our early infancy, hinders our fixing them, and pointing out their characteristical marks. This inconveniency does not take place in things not beginning to exist, or at least not known till after the formation of the language. That language which sees them come into being can characterise them by the most suitable names. Had God permitted a man to have been a spectator of his process in the creation, and to have seen the bodies compose themselves before his face by the coalition of their respective elements, would he not of all men be the best qualified to give us exact descriptions of all natural things, and would not these descriptions greatly surpass all the elaborate publications of chymists, naturalists, and academies, after so many years of assiduous investigation? Now I say, that languages are invested with the like advantages with respect to certain moral relations or combinations, introduced into societies already formed. This I shall prove from marriage.

The common people, it is sufficiently known, have but vague and defective notions concerning it; the ecclesiastical ceremony is all the difference they know of, between marriage and a criminal co-habitation, and this is owing to their being without such a definition as will settle their ideas: but even those of the learned themselves are, on this point, often very faulty: marriage, with them, is a contract for life, with bodily commerce and the breeding of children as its object. If this be a complete definition, I conceive that the magistrate may, under several penalties or a pecuniary fine, prohibit the contracting of marriage without previously solemnizing it, either by the office of the church or some other public ceremony: but he has no right to annul marriages contracted without any of these forms; and in so doing he countervenes the maxims of the Christian religion, by which the conjugal tie is indissoluble, with exception of one case only. As little would he be authorised to invalidate clandestine marriages, contracted against the known inclination of the parents. Our laws in making them void, become contrary to religion; and those English divines who have

charged

charged the act of parliament againſt ſuch marriages as a breach of the law of God, will be in the right *(t)*.

It may perhaps be thought that this definition will be rendered complete and unexceptionable by adding the word *lawful(u)*. If this word be taken in a ſenſe oppoſite to *fraudulent*, real marriage will often be confounded with fornication. Suppoſe, for inſtance, one of the contracting parties, with a view of defrauding the other, ſets up for a fortune beyond what he in reality is poſſeſſed of, this contract unqueſtionably is fraudulent; yet does it conſtitute a marriage; and to go about annulling ſuch contracts, would occaſion difficulties without end.

This definition therefore being manifeſtly deficient, let us ſee wherein its defect lies, and how it may be amended. A man and a woman enter into an agreement to live together, and to bring up the children which ſhall be born by ſuch cohabitation; ſome gallants, in the mean time, are for ſeducing the woman, or even attempt to carry her off: the man has no right to oppoſe them, nor can he, without going beyond an allowable defence, either make uſe of violence againſt the ſeducers, detain the woman againſt her will, or in any wiſe compel her to make good her engagement. That ſhe is in the wrong to break her promiſes I allow; but it is not for him to do himſelf juſtice; as a member of ſociety, he is to ſet down quietly under this diſturbance of his amour, and not break the public peace. On the other hand, the magiſtracy owes him no protection, as having never taken on themſelves the guaranty of ſuch contract. I aſk, whether this can be called a marriage? No, it is evidently no more than concubinage, to which nothing of what laws, either divine or human, have preſcribed, concerning the indiſſolubility of matrimonial engagements is applicable. Hence I perceive what muſt be added to the definition to make it complete: marriage is not barely a contract, but *a contract entered into under the protection and the guaranty of the laws*. In the ſtate of nature,

---

(*t*) See *An Enquiry into the force and operation of the annulling clauſes in a late act for the better preventing of clandeſtine marriages*, London, 1754. Dr. Stebbing's *Diſſertation on the powers of ſtates to deny civil protection to the marriages of minors, made without the conſent of the parents.*

(*u*) The German word is rechtmæſſig, *i. e.* legal, juſt.

as being without laws, marriage is a contract, in the support and maintenance of which *force may be justly used*.

The Greeks had a word which comprised the whole of this definition: this word(*x*) equally signified both marriage and the law; *to be married to one, and to be joined to him by law*, were synonimous expressions. This arose from the Greek tongue being of a more antient date than the custom of marriage, a custom with which the Athenians were utterly unacquainted till the time of Cecrops, and before him it was only the mothers of children who were known. Cecrops was the first who introduced marriage among that rude people; and then it was manifest to every one that marriage is an intercourse of the two sexes, approved of and secured by the laws.

The like happy idiom is found in our language, and not improbably from the like cause. In old German, *law* was called *Ee* or *Eh*, that very word which now signifies marriage. The English, though they have the word marriage, yet to express the French word *gendre*, use an expression which bespeaks the like origin, and may be literally rendered son *according to law*, that is, *son by marriage (y)*. But this very example leads me to a disagreeable remark. To the generality, the treasure of truths hidden in etymology is lost, either from the primitive meaning of the words becoming obsolete, or that since annexed to them, so common, that the etymology is not longer discernible, and they are looked on as no more than arbitrary signs. Without having particularly studied philology and Germanic antiquities, or having turned over old books and records drawn up in the German language, the word *eh* will never be known to have antiently signified a law. In England every body knows the meaning of *law*, but at hearing the words *son in law*, that meaning does not recur to the mind, and the word to a native of England conveys only the import of the French word *gendre*, or a son by *marriage*: thus the etymology does not lay open the

---

(*x*) Νομος. See M. Elsner and M. Carpzow's Commentaries on Romans c. vii. v. 1. Not that I approve of their exposition: I only refer to it on account of their proofs for this signification of the word νόμος, which is none of the most usual τῶ ζῶντι ἀνδρὶ δὲ δέται νόμῳ in the following verses is indisputably a periphrastical definition of marriage.

(*y*) Son-in-law.

truth which it includes. We do not find that either the apologists or antagonists of the *marriage-act* ever in the least thought that the marriage spoken of by Jesus Christ, in the 5th chapter of St. Mathew, requires the guaranty of the laws, and that consequently, what he says of it is not to be applied to concubinage. The words Νομος and γάμος νομιμος, might give the Greeks a clearer insight into this article: they were not become of such common use as to hide their etymologies, γάμος alone being the word ordinarily used.

Many of the terms of our living languages are become so familiar to us, that their derivation escapes us; but with dead languages it is otherwise, as we make use of them more rarely, the etymological truths latent in them are not so easily lost; besides we are better acquainted with their etymologies, as being a branch of literature. This it is that makes us so apt to think their etymologies more significant, and their nomenclature more proper; in short, to give them the preference above living languages, which perhaps is more than they can absolutely claim. In these judgments there is always some partiality; we esteem the sciences according to the time and trouble the acquisition of them cost us; but the more this foible, so common throughout the learned world, swells the encomiums lavished on the dead languages, the greater suspicion it brings on those elogiums. I thought it my duty to declare against this injustice to our mother tongues.

SECTION.

SECTION III.

The names given to things often tend to create love or hatred of them, as representing them either good or evil, and this again is a striking influence of the language on opinions.

THE inoculation of the small pox is an expression quite indifferent, only descriptive of the operation, without raising any prejudice for or against it. Had this insertion been called the *Turkish or Tartarian small pox*, from the countries where it had its origin, it would certainly have met with much greater opposition, so as, perhaps, not to have got footing; and, on the other hand, had it been named *a stratagem against the small pox*, or some such alluring appellation, it would not be so exclaimed against, at least not be looked on as a crime. In a word, were inoculation stiled *the preserver of beauty*, as, if I mistake not, the Circassians call the small pox *the enemy of beauty*; opinions would be divided, the fair sex would cry up inoculation, and gloomy moralists loaded it with invectives.

Whilst scholars and legislators overlook such artifices, the bulk of a people and parental fondness, which nothing escapes, take advantage of such deficiency. The German peasant mentions thunder with an epithet which tends to abate terror, representing it as a benefit (*y*), which likewise is not improper, as in reality fertilizing the country. Some provinces use similar expression: *The good old man is passing along the air* (*z*); the good old man is God, and his passing along the air is the thunder.

To this propriety may be referred even the custom of those languages, in which the name of the Supreme Being is taken from the attribute of goodness. That this is the case of the German word *Gott* is well known;

(*y*) Das liebe Gewitter, i. e. *the dear thunder*; if I may be allowed this Germanism.
(*z*) *Der gute Alte fæhret*.

known; but, in the Hebrew, it is still more remarkable. In several eastern languages God was represented as an object of terror (*a*), and it might be to prevent the pernicious influences of such a representation, that the Hebrew tongue has adopted the word *El*, which is peculiar to it, and quite foreign from the other oriental languages. This name is derived from a word signifying beneficence (*b*), and conveys the idea of a beneficent God. I am very well aware, that commonly a different etymology is given to it; but, in my opinion, erroneously (*c*).

All this does not, however, hinder but that it may often be right for a language to have indifferent names, in which no judgment is implied, no accessory idea conveyed to the mind. The opinion of the first nomenclator may have been an error or prejudice, and by means of the language, this prejudice spreads, which is not the case when there is a neutral or indifferent word for expressing the same thing.

Accessory ideas often operate in a manner still more latent. A word likewise has often several significations, and we, chusing that which is not applicable to the subject in question, are unawares drawn into errors: therefore, to have neutral, or, if I may be allowed the phrase, perfectly impartial terms, implying no secondary idea of either blame or praise is an advantage. Here is a proof of it, which, at the same time, gives me an

---

(*a*) פחד Gen. xxxi. 53. מורא Pf. lxxvi. 12. אימים Jer. l. 38. מפלת 1 Reg. xv. 13. Pf. xl. 5. and in the Syriac text *Ersho*. A modern learned writer has even derived from terror the most usual appellation of God among the Hebrews, that of אלה.

Concerning this see Mr. Michaelis's work, *On the Methods used for understanding the antient Hebrew*, which together with Mr. Hume's *natural history of Religion*, will afford a considerable supplement to the remarks contained in this first section.

(*b*) אלי

(*c*) Aquila translates אל the *mighty God*, and though his authority be not of the greatest weight, he has been followed by the generality of French, English, Danish, and Swedish expositors. Even the German catechism has fallen into this mistake, though Luther had guarded against it, in his version of the Bible. They who render it the *mighty God*, deduce this word from the root איל, whereas the rules of grammar will scarce admit of such a derivation. 1. Because in the word אליערד no vowel appears under the letter א. 2. Because whenever that word denotes the Deity, it is not written איל but אל, without *Jod*.

opportunity of congratulating my mother tongue on some pre-eminences which it has above the Latin.

The supreme, or, as some chuse to term it, the ultimate good, that good to which all others are subservient, as the means are so the ends; and no farther good, than in their relation to it. This good, I say, Epicurus placed in pleasurable sensations; but, as the Latin word for such sensation equally denoted voluptuousness, it conveyed an accessary idea of a softness or luxury scarce compatible with virtue or courage. Can it be doubted but that, in this view, Epicurus's doctrine must have appeared to many Romans, not only ill grounded, but even contemptible and execrable; and yet this was no more than a misunderstanding, owing to a deficiency in the Latin tongue: this Cicero's declamations, which are full of ambiguities, sufficiently prove. The Latin word ever conveyed the idea of voluptuousness; and what success could a philosophy, which esteemed voluptuousness as the supreme good, and as the ultimate end of all our actions, promise itself among a people who was scarce acquainted with any other virtues than the military, or any other pleasures than carnage and victory.

What epicures termed *voluptas*, our language would have called *pleasureable sensation*, leaving no ambiguity, and this denomination would have given no offence either to the austere moralist, or the brave warrior. Suppose I put this question to a man; " how is it that certain things appear to
" us goods, and other evils? that we eagerly pursue some, and as eagerly
" shun others? you desire glory, health, and cheerfulness, is it not so?
" you avoid contempt, pain, sickness, and melancholy, and will never
" willingly expose yourself to these situations, unless occasionally and con-
" sidered as means for averting a greater evil, or obtaining a good which is
" more than an equivalent to these evils. What is the cause of your de-
" sires? This cause or that by reason of which objects wearing the
" aspect of good, please us is called the supreme good, the ultimate
" good, or the end of goods. Now, I say, that this good is reducible to
" a pleasurable sensation, a sensation which admits of no farther analysis,
" which has no connection with any end beyond it, and with which the
" soul

" foul is pleasurably affected, without knowing wherefore. But we know
" that the greater the fum of thefe fenfations, the more we have of them
" in a given time, and the more intenfe and lafting they are, the greater
" our happinefs: that it is only multiplying thefe three quantities, the fum,
" the intenfenefs, and the duration one by the other, and the refult gives you
" the true greatnefs of the good." He to whom I fhall have explained
myfelf in fuch a manner, will be eafily convinced, and I fhall not meet
with that chicanery and abufe which the Roman orator threw out fo very
illiberally againft the Grecian philofopher, not that I, by any means, pretend to ftand forth as an apologift of Epicurus, or maintain that his difci-
ples, and perhaps himfelf, deceived by the ambiguity, may not fometimes have confounded the pleafurable fenfation with voluptuoufnefs.

A copioufnefs of fit words for denoting all the works of nature,
and of art, and whatever relates to morals; in a word, whatever may
come into the mind of the fcholar and the plebeian, and thofe words, not
borrowed from a foreign language; fuch a copioufnefs muft neceffarily be
of great fervice for the improvement of fciences. Objects without a name
feldom fix our attention, whereas thofe which are diftinguifhed by appellations, leave lafting impreffions on us: many are the differences which the
deaf overlook: their attention to thofe of trees and plants, which have fome
refemblance, will not be fo exact as in him who is converfant with the
language. The want of expreffions produces a like effect, and the copioufnefs of them acts contrarily. Where a language is rich it imports
a tincture of knowledge even to the common man: things become known
to him, which without the affiftance of his language he would ever have
remained ignorant of; he obferves the courfe of nature better, and finds
himfelf capable of communicating experiments to the more learned,
which otherwife would have been loft; yet, fuch as are not always be-
neath their notice. On the other hand, they who have devoted themfelves to the fciences will naturally, and without any premeditated ftudy,
familiarize themfelves in their early youth with many notions, which,
any where elfe, would have coft them much clofe application, even in a
more advanced age.

What

What an advantage would it be to us had all vegetables German names, equally known to the people and the naturalists? What an ease would this be to the study of Botany? the memory would then be relieved from the load of a crabbed Nomenclature; which at least makes one half of the elements of that science; the names of the vegetables being already known to us, the whole business would be to remember their figure. What a difficulty is the lover of Botany put to in learning that multitude of foreign appellations, which with their Greek or Latin terminations disgust his ear? especially if, which is frequently the case, he is not such a master of those languages, as to be able to help himself by means of the etymology.

The Greeks and Latins, it must be owned, had conveniences which are wanting to us; but as they out-do us in this respect, they are no less out-done by the Orientals. The richness of the Arabic and Hebrew comes little short of that of nature itself. Every individual product of nature, in those countries, has a name taken from the particular stock of those languages, and these names are so frequently made use of by the very poets, and in books of mere entertainment, that the literati and the wits could not well be ignorant of them; even they who did not make natural history their study, met with them in their reading, and they, as it were, obtruded themselves on them in their closets.

Such a happy constitution of the national language, not only saves the professed Botanist much time and trouble, but the people in general shall be better acquainted with the works of nature than we are. There will scarce be any one without some superficial knowledge of the vegetable kingdom: curiosity animated by leisure, and the facility of gratifying itself, will endeavour after improvements, and the number of intelligent Botanists will increase. The gardener and the rustic, understanding those Adepts, will bestow more attention on natural productions, and thus come to be a kind of connoisseurs. Omitting the increase of wisdom and happiness in a nation, as it improves in knowledge, it is sufficient for my purpose that Botany is improved there. In Germany, for one real Botanist, we may, at any time, reckon a thousand persons who have not the least idea of that science: they walk about in the fields, amidst a rich display of nature's various productions, but they are blind, and are so only for want of fit words to diftinguifh the productions. Yet, can it be denied that, were this impediment removed, more difcoveries might not be expected from thefe thoufand men than can be hoped for from the application of a fingle Botanift? It is a queftion, whether the difcovery of effects of plants, both falutary and noxious, and the human and animal fpecies are lefs owing to accident than to inveftigation; and he to whofe eyes the operations of nature continually prefent themfelves fhall fooner hit on this chance, than he who only now and then beftows an excurfion of a few hours in prying into them. But of what ufe will that important accident be to the former, if ignorant of what he fhould attend to, if unacquainted with the diftinction of plants, if he looks on them only as an infignificant part of that variegated carpet with which the furface of the earth is covered?

Though I cannot fay that the before-mentioned nations have availed themfelves of that fuperiority of their languages fo far as they might; yet to me it appears out of all queftion, that the vegetable kingdom was better known to the antient eaftern literati, than it is to the modern. For this I only appeal to the books of the Old Teftament, the fubject of which is either hiftorical or theological, and which were written with quite another view than teaching Botany, and yet they furnifh us with above two hundred and fifty names of vegetables: now the writers who have made ufe of thofe names both in profe and metre, were not Botanifts by profeffion, that in all probability, fuch kind of knowledge muft in thofe times have been very common.

In order to fet the advantages of fuch languages in a ftill clearer light, and point out the methods by which others may obtain the like advantages, I fhall examine the caufes of the want of them in the German. It is not its poverty, being intrinfically very rich, that any impoverifhment of it muft be partly imputed even to its very richnefs, and partly to an extreme degeneracy in thofe who fpeak it.

I afk a peafant the name of a plant; he tells me it has no name; now even this is no proof of the poverty of the language; it may only fhew the peafant's ignorance, or that of his whole village, or of his diftrict. How can it be thought that the treafure of botanical terms fhould be preferved among the

loweft

lowest class of mankind, among the poor cottagers, who harrassed with labour and distress, cannot be supposed to advert much to things from which they neither expect good or harm. I then apply to a Botanist, and he sends me away with a Latin word; he knows no other; nay, he knows not so much as the German names of several plants, which any peasant could tell me. From all this it does not, however, follow that the plant in hand has absolutely no name; it may perhaps be met with in some province of Germany; but lying dormant there, and being still less known to the learned, it is of no use to the sciences, and might as well not exist. Things grow continually worse and worse; the country people succeslively forget some of these names, which are so many losses, the continuance of which impoverish a language. These words beingun known to the learned, cannot be preserved in their works. Several vegetables are proscribed by poetry, and cannot gain admittance, neither under their popular names, nor under the technical denominations. The former are too mean, the latter have an uncouth sound, or would disorder the cadence of the line.

Visit the different countries of Germany, and instead of complaining of the want of names, you will rather complain of a super-abundance, and its great inconveniencies. You will find that the plant which you imagine to have no name has several, but they are only provincial names. The language of the inhabitants of Miznia is Hebrew to the Swisser, and as little does the Leipziger understand that of Lower Saxony: nay, what is much more, I have myself seen Botanists of great reputation, reject the German names of certain plants as barbarous, finding fault with those that use them, and advising them to substitute Latin terms, yet those German names go current at Leipzig and its environs, both among the commonalty and the gentry: and if this city be in reality the seat of the German language, they could not be reckoned provincial or country words, that if not understood, the fault was in the readers, and not in the writers.

And whence comes it that they are so little understood? The whole blame lies on our Botanists, who are so infatuated with the Latin nomenclature, so far as to exclude that of their own country, and even blame the use of it. Other literati do the like, the less affinity an expression has with the

German, in their eſtimate, the more elegant, the more it captivates them under the parade of erudition ; our vernacular expreſſions they baniſh to the villages, pronouncing them coarſe and mean, and vilifying them till they have quite exploded them out of the language. What are we the better in having, for inſtance, three or four names for the ſame plant, when neither of them can come to be claſſical ; now this is an honour no name can attain till ſome famous Botaniſt ſhall make uſe of it both in his writings and lectures, leaving to the Latin word the inferior office of explaining it, whereas it is directly the contrary : the explanatory part is ſometimes aſſigned to the German name, and even this is reckoned as no ſmall favour done to it.

It will perhaps be ſaid that the import of the Latin names is more fixed and definitive; but that is manifeſtly falſe, without diſtorting the ſenſe from that which they bear in pure Latin; and if that be all, I do not ſee why the import of the German terms may not be changed for an artificial one adapted to the ſyſtem.

This therefore is not the real cauſe why our Botaniſts ſpeak Latin; it lies in a fantaſtical mode, which has crept into the German univerſities. The uſing Latin, which the other faculties have almoſt every where departed from in their lectures, is ſtill retained in phyſic, and without any apparent reaſon, the ſtudents in phyſic being generally, of any other claſs, the leaſt acquainted with Latin. Botany, however, accounted a branch of phyſic, is taught in Latin, and the auditors know of no other terms than thoſe they have learned from their maſters.

Though I am very far from the leaſt thought of contributing to exclude the Latin tongue from the univerſities, I own, I could wiſh, and I think the love of my country warrants ſuch a wiſh, that it would relinquiſh Botany and natural hiſtory to our own language. Let all the other ſciences be taught in Latin; yet be thoſe excepted of which we are partly to collect the materials among the country people : what ſhall we be the better for their diſcoveries, if we do not underſtand their ſpeech ? Beſides, the Latin tongue is very unfit for natural hiſtory : the beſt judges will tell you that with regard to a great number both of vegetables and animals, it is

ſtill

ſtill very uncertain whether they formerly bore thoſe names which the moderns have given them. In ſhort, we have every motive for diſmiſſing the Latin language out of botanical auditories, where it is ſo manifeſtly improper. The many faults committed there againſt proſody, not to ſay againſt grammar, are inſupportable to every Latin ear, and it is ſcarce poſſible but that youth muſt contract a vicious pronunciation. I ſhould therefore think that neither the lovers of Latin or of Botany, would object againſt the ſuppreſſion of ſo fantaſtical and pernicious a cuſtom. I could heartily intreat our Botanical profeſſors, to ſhew their love to their country, ſo far as to deliver their lectures in its language. I remember to have heard one of the moſt eminent among them ſay: that were all Baron Wolfe's other merits diſputed, there was one which muſt inconteſtibly be allowed him, his having added a new degree of perfection to the German tongue, by applying it to philoſophy. Much more neceſſary would it be to apply it to Botany, and much eaſier would be the taſk; it would be only collecting the names of which the language is already poſſeſſed, and this very collection is partly made by the care and diligence of former Botaniſts. It only requires to be made uſe of, and certainly it would not long remain neglected, did we conſider that to improve our language is really augmenting our national ſtock of knowledge and wiſdom. The riches of nature are loſt to thoſe who know not how to name them; whereas give them names derived from the language of the country, and they will be taken notice of by multitudes, who otherwiſe ſcarce caſt an eye on them or very ſuperficially. Many other wiſhes could I mention, would bare wiſhes do. I could wiſh, for inſtance, that we had German names for whole claſſes, as for *Monandria, Diandria*, &c. theſe names when once in vogue, would greatly facilitate the Botanical ſyſtems, and bring them within the capacity of the moſt illiterate; the ſenſe of them would be got amidſt diverſions, and in our walks. I could likewiſe wiſh that each conſtituent part of vegetables had its particular term. The Orientals have a diſtinct word for expreſſing the *virgin-herb,* and another for the *fecundated-herb* (*e*), which certainly is to the praiſe of their language.

(*e*) *Herba virgo & maritata*, the former is called רשא the latter בעל.

Our

[28]

Our language has a great pre-eminence relatively to the mineral kingdom, and whatever concerns *metallurgy* and *mineralogy*, moſt European languages borrowing from it; but infinitely more advantageous would this copiouſneſs be to us could we transfer it to Botany. Mines being but thinly ſown, the terms relating to thoſe ſciences, are, in the greater part of the empire, as little known as if they were Chineſe words: I proceed to other examples.

Our commonalty fill the whole extent from the earth to the firmament with air, and imagine it to be every where the ſame matter. The Greeks could eaſily guard againſt this error; their language diſtinguiſhes the atmoſphere from the *ether*, or celeſtial matter by two diſtinct words, expreſſing thoſe two bodies ſeparately.

Some virtues are more ſeduloufly inculcated by moraliſts and philoſophers when the language has fit names for indicating them; whereas they are but ſuperficially treated of, or rather neglected in nations where ſuch virtues have not ſo much as a name. The antients cried up, and perhaps too highly, that independency of the wiſe man, which renders him ſelf-ſufficient, that his happineſs is not connected with external things. Among the moderns, little or no mention is made of ſuch a quality.

A language abounding in terms which at once denote great numbers, without particularizing the multiplication from which they ariſe, forms the mathematical genius, helping it to repreſent to itſelf very confiderable qualities without any meditation: this is daily ſeen. Every homeſpun ruſtic knows the difference between *thouſand* and *hundred*: and no very cultivated mind, at leaſt no profoundity in geometry is required to comprehend the import of a *hundred thouſand, two hundred thouſand*; but on coming to numbers of which the names are exotic, then it is that we enter on darkneſs. Women, the illiterate, not a few trades people, otherwiſe pretty well acquainted with figures; nay, even ſome literati confound *million* with a *hundred thouſand*: and though you explain the difference of them over and over, it ſoon gives their memory the ſlip. As to billions, trillions, &c. theſe they account inconceivable numbers, that to them

theſe

these words convey only a vague idea of some immense quantity. Now, a mind which, beyond a certain quantity, sees only a confused immensity, the measurement of which overwhelms it, will never make a figure in Geometry.

I shall shew, by five comparisons, how the richness of a language may influence arithmetical ideas, and to this purpose successively compare with our language the condition of a people without a language, a poorer language, a richer language; and lastly, two possible languages.

To form distinct ideas of numbers, beyond what imagination can take in at once, would be extremely difficult, without a language and without emblems to supply the want of it. Some have judged this could not be beyond three; I am inclined to think, that the number of our fingers being continually before our eyes, might raise our conception to five; but it would be hard to fix the idea of any thing above five, and of all multiples of five. He who could conceive five heaps, each of five unities, or the square of five, would be a transcendent genius indeed.

In America there are people who cannot reckon beyond twenty; whatver exceeds that number they compare with that of their hair; a very proper expression for denoting a confused, and, to them, indeterminable quantity: to such, great numbers must appear something, of which no precise idea is to be formed. How far must their mathematical notions be from those of our peasants? the most intelligent, unless endowed with an almost divine genius, or his ideas have been enlarged by instruction, will not come near their conceptions. But other influences must necessarily be the consequences of such incapacity: without some knowledge of figures we continually commit mistakes.

As twenty is to those people a thousand is to us; and we have the additional advantage of multiplication. Our language can say a thousand times a thousand, and likewise reckon the multiples; whereas those Americans know nothing of twenty times twenty, and can indicate their meaning only by the very indefinite token of shewing their hair. This puts me in mind of the king of the *Nine Nations*, to whom the account given him of the inhabitants of London appearing beyond all belief, he ordered his envoy to count them by means of a thread, making a knot for each inhabitant. The envoy finding his commission impracticable, only assured his sovereign that the number of them was equal to that of the hairs of his head, and this he might say without the least hyperbole. Were the story no more than a fiction; still does it very naturally represent the consequences of a poor language, and holds up to us our advantages.

I have said that a *thousand*, which is our last numerical term, may in our language be increased by multiplication; yet this has its limits, and I know not whether many people are capable of forming to themselves a distinct idea beyond a triple repetition of a thousand times, that is beyond a thousand times a thousand times a thousand: for my part, were it carried farther, I should be obliged to have recourse to the foreign technical terms of billion, trillion, &c. or to those of fourth, fifth power, &c. But even these are artificial ideas, entirely owing to instruction, beyond the verge of our language, consequently such as are not to be expected among the bulk of mankind: let any one try to form to himself a clear conception of *a thousand times a thousand times a thousand times a thousand times a thousand times a thousand times a thousand*; I am persuaded that this number will not represent to us a greater quantity than if one of the *thousand times* was omitted; and consequently the total was but a thousandth part of what it is. Let us, on the other hand, suppose that our language could, in simple uncompounded terms express a million, a thousand and thousand times a thousand millions; this it is certain would enable us to form a clear conception of numbers infinitely greater.

In this point the Greeks and Hebrews have the advantage of us, their language expressing ten thousand by one word, the former by *myriad* the latter by *ribbo* (*f*). From thence is composed *myriads* of *myriads*, ten thousand

---

(*f*) Here may be observed the successive gradations of the improvement of languages in numerical words. Names, at first, given to indeterminate numbers, or even to such as were accounted immense, became, as men grew able to compute such numbers, the names of determinate

thoufand times ten thoufand, a number ftrangely perplexing even to men of great learning, that fometimes, by a falfe calculation, they make ten millions when in reality it is a hundred millions, and fometimes it appears to them a number immenfe beyond expreffion. An inftance of this is Luther himfelf, who has fallen into both thefe overfights. In a paffage of the prophet Daniel he mifreckons, and tranflates *ten hundred times a thoufand (g)*; in a paffage of the Revelations, he renders the fame expreffion by the indeterminate quantity of *many thoufand times a thoufand (h)*: thus thofe people were no more at a lofs to conceive a hundred millions than we to conceive one. The Hebrews could even exprefs that immenfe number, by giving the dual termination to the word which among them indicated a myriad (*i*).

How great would be the advantages of a language having, for expreffing numbers, feven fimple words more than we have? We have the names of nine unities, thofe of nine tens reckoned from 10 to 90; and laftly, thofe of the fquare and cube of the number ten, which are *a hundred* and *a thoufand*. Now does not analogy feem to require, that we fhould farther have terms for expreffing the ten firft powers of this num-

---

terminate quantities. Of μυρία, originally fignifying innumerable, has been made μύρια, *ten thoufand*. It is the fame with the Hebrew אלף which means a *thoufand*. It was originally the appellation of a part of a tribe, confifting of a number of families רבבה; or רבו *ten thoufand*, originally denotes *the multitude* in general. Had we brigades of ten thoufand men, the name of fuch a brigade might poffibly have raifed our numerical terms from the third power of number 10 to its fourth power. Incidents of this kind contribute to the improvement of a language more than all the application and genius of the learned.

(*g*) Zehen hundertmal taufend. Dan. VII. 10.
(*h*) Viel taufendmal taufend. Apoc. IX. 16.
(*i*) רבבה, the dual of which is רבותים, or the fquare of ten thoufand. Pf. LXVIII. 18. which to tranflate twice ten thoufand, would be an incongruity; the combining, fo inferior a number with that of a thoufand times a thoufand, would be fomething beyond a poetical licence. The expreffion implying *the thoufands of the re-duplication*, and which in the fame verfe fignifies a thoufand times a thoufand, fufficiently fhews the true meaning of 10,000 in the dual to be the fquare, or fecond power of 10,000.

ber? Were it thus, every one, with the slightest tincture of arithmetic, would as easily conceive ten thousand millions as he at present conceives the number *thousand*, and the square of those ten thousand millions, or 100,000,000,000,000,000,000, would then be to us what the square of a thousand is at present. With the assistance of such a language, there is no body who would not be able to form to himself notions of those magnitudes, which are the objects of astronomical calculations and measurements; notions in which the learned themselves are lost, unless conversant with geometry.

Some eminent mathematicians have proposed binary arithmetic, which consists in making of the number two the very same use now made of the number ten. However plausible this project may appear in one light, yet it certainly tends for to clog and confine geometrical genius, unless its inconvenience be remedied by coining particular names for the number two when carried to very high powers. Its tenth power makes but 1024, which is very little beyond the third power of ten, and to exceed a million, it must be carried to the twentieth power (*k*).

(*k*) The academy could have wished that I had here mentioned Algebra, and mathematical analysis which may be looked on as new languages, the discovery of which has so prodigiously extended the limits of our knowledge. I conceived it became me to keep to the words of the problem, and consequently to speak only of national languages. I, however, allow that this new point of view might lead to many very important truths and discoveries: and this subject well deserves to be thoroughly handled by a geometrical philosopher, to whom Algebra is, as it were, become his second language. For my part I could have spoken but very deficiently on a science which has grown into disuse with me for several years past.

SECTION IV.

The advantageous influences of a language on opinions may be reduced to two heads; copiousness of terms, and fecundity of etymologies and expressions.

I. TO consider the former in all its amplitude and perfection, the idea of it might be carried ad infinitum. Whatever could be thought of must have a name peculiar to itself, and a name both national and clear, and fully expressive of its object without any periphrasis, it should likewise enable the speakers to represent the same object under different points of view, at least, under the two principal, as indifferent, and as beneficial or hurtful, according to its real nature; nay, it would not seldom be necessary that one could even give to objects these three senses equally: that is, when they have an advantageous side, and a side which shews them to disadvantage; such, for instance, is a too uniform, and permanent happiness, by which we contract an insensibility to enjoyments with which we are surrounded.

Such a perfection of language I grant is a mere chimera, never to be realized. The shortness of life, and the limits of our intellects will ever be an insurmountable impediment. The words of such a copious language cannot be repeated often enough to take root, and grow into custom, and it is the words generally known by which opinions can be influenced; those words for which the learned are obliged to consult dictionaries, and which the ignorant do not in the least understand, have no more effect, though taken from the national language, than if they were Latin words.

II. Fecund

II. Fecund etymologies and expressions are such as include many interesting truths: but these expressions must not be over common: amidst a too frequent use of them, their useful part would escape our attention.

It is needless to declare that there is no language of any such perfection; they are all the work of imperfect men; and the Fables of the Jews, who are for making the Hebrew a language all divine, have been sufficiently confuted by unexceptionable judges.

All the treasures of knowledge yet to be met with, in any language have been brought into it by individuals; they are all owing either to serious invention, or the sudden fruits of festivity and chance.

SUPPLEMENT I.

The academy, as I see by the extract which has been made of my dissertation, could have wished that I had begun my second part by a general dissertation, establishing the preference of language to all other imaginable ways of communicating one's ideas, and examining the proportion between the degrees of genius, understanding, and knowledge of nations, on one hand, and on the other between the greater or lesser richness of their different languages.

I would willingly repair this omission did time permit, and did I not believe that I should spare it for more important additions.

I do not, however, apprehend, that the reader will be any great loser by the omission: all that relates to general reasonings, he will find in the books of those philosophers who treat of the symbolic part of our knowledge; and as to proofs of fact, this piece is not wanting in them.

They who were deaf at their birth, are deplorably stupid; whereas they who were born blind, often shew a capacity and penetration much above the common. This difference can proceed only from the use of speech, which is wanting to the former, and which the latter enjoys. A stranger, on coming into a very populous city, is at first hard put to it to imprint on his imagination

gination and memory, the several countenances of the inhabitants; but whenever he comes to know their names, he easily remembers and distinguishes them; an evident proof how very much our thoughts are influenced by these symbols, whereas it is but very slowly that we come to distinguish similar things, for which we know no name. The impressions of the senses soon pass away; it is only by means of the names annexed to them that the human mind recalls their fleeting images; and the mind seems naturally disposed to associate ideas to sounds. He who can conceive abstract ideas, without the help of signs, must be an extraordinary genius indeed, and it is beyond even his abilities, when these ideas are very complicated: of this transcendant geometry affords numberless proofs. I may one day enlarge on this subject, in treating of the origin of languages.

The comparison of nations concerning the proportion of their knowledge to their language, besides surpassing my abilities, would expose me to give great offence in the execution. I shall, however, take the liberty of mentioning the following observations.

A capacity of making such comparisons requires that one be perfectly acquainted with the languages of those nations, the intellects of which have hitherto made no great progress; but here it is that the difficulty lies. This cannot be referred to those very nations, every one usually siding with his mother tongue, and would make up its deficiency by extravagant praises. A foreigner, from whom more impartiality may be expected, is little disposed to apply himself to a language which he does not foresee will furnish him with much useful knowledge; and a philosopher learns only those which have produced many excellent works. It being my intention thoroughly to digest the subject, recommended to me by the academy, it would give me infinite pleasure to meet with accurate and impartial accounts of the degree of perfection, or imperfection of the languages of certain nations, whose genius and knowledge are still very narrow: to name those would be a breach in manners; but that there are such languages in Europe, is unquestionable, especially if we take into the account idioms, known only in the country, and among the commonality.

The

The fureſt method for determining the richneſs of languages is by tranſlations. Thoſe which are poor, will ſoon betray their indigence; if ſome work with variety of matter, and written in a rich language, be attempted to be rendered into them: the tranſlator will be reduced to have recourſe ſometimes to Latin terms, ſometimes to long paraphraſes, and will often mutilate a thought. This rule may, however, fail in the hands of a bad tranſlator, who either is not acquainted with the ſubject, or not verſed in his own language, or laſtly, has not that quickneſs and verſatility required for hitting and tranſlating all the ideas and terms of the original: in a word, if the tranſlators be ſuch as our German bookſellers generally employ.

The richneſs or poverty of a language can ſcarce be abſolutely determined. Languages are generally rich or poor, only with regard to certain objects; that which abounds with philoſophic expreſſions, may be very barren in all the appurtenances of ſhip-building and navigation: this would neceſſarily be the caſe of the Swiſſers, had they a peculiar national language. Several analogous inſtances will be met with in this treatiſe.

The moſt enlightened nations of Europe, the Germans, the French, the Engliſh, and the Italians, differ ſo little, either in the richneſs of their languages, or the ſtock of national knowledge, that the more and the leſs cannot be determined without great riſk of being miſtaken. Dimenſions which do not come within geometrical menſuration, cannot be compared, unleſs their difference be palpable. We will, therefore, allow the Engliſh, and that is the fartheſt we can go, that their language is the richeſt, and they themſelves, without breach of modeſty, aſſert that advantage; for beſides its being a mixture of three different languages, it not only is continually enriching itſelf with ſpoils from the Latin and French, but it farther allows of coining new words, and yet I am not without ſome doubts on the reality of their advantage. I never found it impoſſible, or even very difficult to tranſlate Engliſh pieces into German, or to concentrate the ſubſtance of them in extracts, abridging the thoughts, yet preſerving all their perſpicuity, and this without borrowing a ſingle foreign word. Neither do French tranſlators ſeem more at a loſs; but of this I am am lefs qualified to judge, than of the language into which I myfelf have tranflated Englifh.

Laftly, When literate nations are to be compared, we muft carefully diftinguifh thofe which produce a great number of fcholars, or at leaft nominal fcholars, from thofe where knowledge is more diffufed among the bulk of the nation; I mean where the officers, country gentlemen, and farmers, &c. have a greater fhare of tafte, and more knowledge than in other parts. This laft circumftance ever bears a greater proportion to the richnefs of a language than the former. A fcholar by profeflion, far from confining himfelf to his natural language, converfes with the Greek and the Latin, and the living languages: that, how bad and poor foever his own language may be, he attains the fame degree of knowledge as the learned, whofe mother tongues are of an univerfal richnefs, provided he makes up this difadvantage by affiduous application. There may be great Botanifts among a people, though they have but few terms belonging to the vegetable kingdom. This indeed is not impoffible, but where the Botanic language is rich, our younger years receive a tincture of it, that in youth we the more eafily acquire a regular knowledge of the fcience.

SUPPLEMENT II.

Since my committing the above reflections to paper, I have been in company with a perfon, of all the world the moft capable of furnifhing us with the neceffary helps for eftimating the proportion between the knowledge of the feveral nations and their refpective languages, I mean Mr. Buttner, a profeffor in the univerfity of Gottingen *(1)*. This learned

(1) There being at prefent two profeffors of that name at Gottingen, both Botanifts, and who have both vifited France, it may not be amifs to inform the reader, that the perfon here intended is Mr. William Buttner, profeffor extraordinary, a native of Wolfenbuttle, very well known to moft of the French officers of diftinction who were in garrifon here, or who paffed through this city, being frequently vifited by them on account of his fine collection of natural curiofities.

gentleman

gentleman, whose knowledge is as profound as general, is about a Polyglot work, far surpassing that of Chamberlayne. In one column he couches the Latin terms, according to the order of the sciences and arts; in the others, he places the words answerable to them, in the other languages. Thus, at one view exhibiting the comparative copiousness and indigence of all those languages, and farther distinguishing what is the original property of each, from its borrowed stores.

Two men of letters were likewise in company with us, one a native of Strasburg, who as such may in some measure be looked on as both French and German; the other, a Frenchman, but very conversant with our language. Before this kind of tribunal of our own setting up, we brought the languages of the several nations, in order to an examination of their merits and defects.

We all unanimously agreed that the German is a very rich language, infinitely richer than the French.

On interrogating Mr. Buttner, our common friend, concerning some languages which we did not understand, the substance of his answers, and those of his dictionary, which we consulted at the same time was as follows:

The Hungarian language is very poor, and its terms of art it borrows from the Sclavonian.

The Russian, the Polish, the Bohemian, the Vandalian, the Sclavonian, being but one and the same language, the Sclavonian dialect as spoken in Lusatia, is the very poorest of all those idioms, and indeed it cannot be otherwise, being only the dialect of mean rustics, without so much as one single book written in it. The Russian language, on the contrary, is the richest, it abounds especially in philosophic terms, which I conjectured might have been introduced from the Greek languages, by the channel of theological controversies, and Mr. Buttner found my conjecture verified by experience. One would at first be inclined to think that the Polish language should be richer than the Russian, yet it is otherwise; and if I am not mistaken, one thing that keeps it thus poor, is the very frequent use of Latin in Poland.

I asked

I asked whether the Russians had any mineralogic terms? the answer was, that they had none properly their own, and that they adopted the German terms. This I was not surprized at, as from us they learned to work mines. But my wonder is that our language should be so very copious in all the concerns of mineralogy, as in Tacitus's time we had not looked into the bowels of the earth. The age of the Otho's stands happily signalized for having both discovered metals, and enriched the language: besides it is not common that a people of itself invents names for new objects; they naturally borrow them from the nations which brought them acquainted with such objects. I should be very desirous of knowing whether the Vandals and Sclavonians, settled in Germany and in Hungary, along both sides of the Danube, a country full of mines, whether I say they have mineralogic terms of their own, or whether they borrowed those of the Germans.

The Bohemian language, said Mr. Buttner, is absolutely void of sea-terms, and the Russians make use of ours. The reason of this is obvious.

But what was quite new and very unexpected, we found the Danish to be one of the poorest languages of any spoken in Europe, and particularly much poorer than the Swedish, with which it has such an affinity. If this be the real case, it seems an indisputable proof that the richness of national knowledge is not always proportioned to the richness of the language, for that literature and science have long since flourished in Denmark, is what cannot be denied. The want of knowledge is not the only cause of the poverty of languages; there are others, and I think I have hit on them. The national language is impoverished by the learned languages coming too much into vogue, especially if the writers of that nation prefer them to their own. In Denmark there are, as it were, two learned languages; the Latin and the German; the latter is become so general there, that many Danes look on it as a second mother tongue, that it is not at all surprising, the language of that country should be so defective: under such a contemptuous neglect, it must necessarily want many terms and expressions, and gradually lose no small part of its present stock, scanty as it is.

SECTION

SECTION V.

Bad influences of a language on opinions.

LANGUAGES may do hurt several ways, which I reduce to six, 1st. By their poverty. 2d. By copiousness. 3d. By equivocations. 4th. By accessory ideas and false judgments, inseparable from the principal idea. 5th. By etymologies and expressions, pregnant with errors, or productive of mistakes. 6th. By an overweening fondness for certain arbitrary beauties.

POVERTY.

We have seen above the instance of the Ethiopians, who having but one word for both *person* and for *nature*, could not comprehend the doctrine of the union of Christ's two natures in one single person.

We have likewise seen that among the Greeks and Romans, the Deity had no peculiar identical name, and to this may probably be imputed the badness of their philosophy, and their defectuous notions in every thing relating to theology. And this it was which made their most eminent geniuses so fluctuating and uncertain concerning the question, *Whether there are Gods*. Whereas among us it will not be easy to find a sensible man, even though an infidel in point of religion, who questions the existence of the Deity. But the wretched reasoning of the ancients on that important head, proceeded from this: they never formed the question, *Is there a God?* by itself. They always added the following; *Are there angels? Are there Genii, whose power and wisdom surpass the power and wisdom of men?* This last question was what philosophy could not resolve: wanting

the

the light of revelation, it had nothing to adduce on this head beyond very weak proofs *a priori*, aud some accounts of pretended apparitions, which would not bear examining. It is therefore not at all strange that they should have fluctuated amidst doubts, whilst no body exhorted them, according to the form used in the Roman senate, to divide their opinion (*m*), and that Unitarians, or they who worshipped only one God, were looked on as no Atheists. The very plural of the Latin word for God (*Dii*) which was so frequently in their mouth, hindered them from separating two questions so very different: finite and contracted as their Deities were, a fresh confusion led them to attribute indiscriminately to the whole tribe of Deities, infinitude, supreme felicity, and omniscience. Looking on these properties as inseparable, from the notion of a God, whatever he might be (*n*); though a direct contradiction to the plurality of them, which took its rise only from their not thinking one single God sufficient for the creation and government of the universe.

Here I recollect that some divines have censured all languages as deficient, not one being able to express all the divine things without throwing us into confusion. This I allow in things of which we have no ideas, or at least only negative ideas; for instance, of infinitude, or concerning the manner in which omnipotence acts, without contact or pulsation, but by bare volition; and this both on mundane objects, and non-entity itself; or lastly, of the precise cause of the necessity of his existence. The having in one's self the foundation of one's essence, is to be sure an incomprehensible expression; but instead of charging it on the poverty of languages, it is that of our mind, which is to be lamented. Is it not quite unreasonable to expect that human languages shall express what the human mind cannot conceive? One might indeed, in imitation of the Algebraists, who denote the unknown qualities of which they are seeking the worth, by $X\ Y\ Z$, one might, I say, to denote divine things, make use of every sound which hitherto has no sense annexed to it, but

---

(*m*) Divide sententiam.
(*n*) Cicero de natura Deorum. lib. 1. sect. 27, 28.

but where would be the advantage of this? Should we be better acquainted with the objects indicated by these sounds. But this, however, is not properly what is complained of: it were to be wished, say they, that languages had expressions less harsh, and more exact for expressing certain truths, for instance these: *God has not a right to break his promises. He has not a right to predestinate us, absolutely and unconditionally to an eternal misery, as this would efface the kindness of creation, and render nihility preferable to existence. God cannot sin nor lie, nor realize contradictions.* It is, these modes of expressions that offend; for God, say they, can do every thing, and it would be absurd to deny him any right or prerogative. I have lately, a second time, met with these complaints in the work of a very judicious writer, where I should not have expected them(n), but it is only from a zeal wanting knowledge that they proceed: these expressions are not at all harsh, and what they give to understand is the very truth.

The instance of Botany has in the preceding section shewn us what a detriment the poverty of language is to natural history. This is a defect not to be remedied either by scientific names, taken from the language of the learned, nor by definitions. 1. These definitions and these names differ still more from one another than the country names. Every literator has a right of changing them at his pleasure, and to secure this precious right, never fails making use of it as often as he can. 2. These names are known only to those who make natural history their business, and thus like the hieroglyphical figures of the Egyptians, they serve only to conceal the most useful discoveries from the knowledge of all the rest of mankind. How should the peasant, the shepherd, the miner, the traveller distinguish, and much less make observations on objects, of which they know not the names? 3. What few observations nature will, as I may say, oblige them to make, are lost to the academic naturalist, they not being able to explain them to him in his idiom. 4. Foreign

---

(n) *Observ. Miscell. in Librum, Job,* page 317, 318. Ed. d'Amst. 1758. The journalists have justly praised the philosophic cast which distinguishes this composition.

reign words and technical terms not being current in common life, are the more difficult to retain, and the study of them the more irkfome. - 5. They are excluded from poetry, which is no fmall difadvantage. It is through poetry that natural hiftory gains admittance into the clofets of thofe who do not trouble themfelves about going after it in the fields, or in the abyffes of the earth. When a picture has charmed us in poetry, we are curious to fee the original, and on feeing it, memory faithfully retains the impreffion.

COPIOUSNESS.

Copioufnefs feldom proves hurtful, but when for want of being proportionally diftributed, it happens to be joined with a fcarcity in the fame kind of expreffions. Suppofe, for inftance, that two different names are given to two vegetables, which, from their very near refemblance fhould, according to the analogy of the language, have but one; or that two are given to two fpecies of the fame kind, which every where elfe are diftinguifhed only by the addition of an adjective to the generical name, or by compofition (*p*). What is the confequence? The people will imagine thefe two vegetables to be abfolutely different, and will never apprehend that they can produce the fame effects, and anfwer the fame ends. Perhaps, and then the miftake will be ftill the more grofs, they will make two kinds of them; but this would be an error, owing to etymology.

The affluence of fynonimes fwells vocabularies; but provided that thefe fynonimes be every where underftood, it is fo far from being a detriment to languages, that it rather embellifhes them by variety of expreffions. Synonimes do no hurt but when fcattered in different provinces; as then by this unhappy copioufnefs the fame people do not under-

---

(*p*) As in Germany, adding an adjective, we fay, *Weiffe Tanne*, and otherwife by compofition; *Edel-Tanne*; which is a kind of pine. Tanne alone, properly, fignifying a fir-tree.

ftand

stand one another, any more than if they spoke two different languages; natural history especially suffers by it. But it is much worse when two synonimes go current at once in two provinces, under different significations. Such, I am told, is the case of the German words which denote the fir and pine-tree (*q*). The only remedy is to make one of these two names classical, and this honour should be conferred on the province producing some great Naturalists who, at the same time, must be a writer of such weight, as to give currency to a word. To oppose this would be a very mistaken zeal for one's province; the love of one's common country, and that of the sciences is to preponderate. Besides, all oppositions must soon fall before his authority. Classical authors are the conquerors of the empire of languages be their cause right or wrong, they always carry the day.

When the other provincial names can be applied to lower species, which till then had gone without a name, a copiousness, so hurtful in itself, becomes turned to a use still more happy and beneficial.

EQUIVOCATION.

All homonymies are not equivocations, and consequently not to be condemned indiscriminately. Homonomy often does good service to languages. It helps the memory, it pleases the imagination, which delights in resemblances, and it relieves the understanding, whereas jejune writers, and others, servilely adhering to the propriety of the meaning, disgust the reader. Proscribing it would signify nothing; our fondness for the figurative stile would be continually bringing it into vogue. When between objects of the same name, there is no inconsiderable difference, and this difference is sufficiently pointed out in the connection of the discourse, so as not to be confounded, no equivocation need be apprehended. When the Latins met with the word *Lupus* in a passage relating to carrying off sheep; it is not to be thought that they could imagine the sheep had

(*q*) *Fichte* and *Tanne*.

been

been carried off by a pike, and in as little danger are we of confounding the celeſtial bear with the terreſtrial animal, from which the former derives its name. When the name of God is given to ſuperior intelligences, their inviſibility, their grandeur, and the awe they inſpire, make them appear not a little different from any thing we are acquainted with, and give them ſuch a reſemblance with the Deity as may lead us into monſtrous errors; whereas we never ſhall be ſo far miſled by the poets beſtowing this title on worldly monarchs, knowing them to be of the ſame nature with ourſelves. All are agreed in the eſſential difference to be made between the proper ſenſe of a word, and its figurative, ſublime, and poetical import.

It is therefore a capital rule that *homonymy is dangerous only when different objects denoted by the ſame name have ſo near a reſemblance, or are ſo intimately connected, as to be eaſily miſtaken for one another.*

But nature has taken care that this ſhall not be the caſe too frequently, by giving us a predilection for thoſe bold figures in which the expreſſions are ſo remote from their common meaning, that it is impoſſible we ſhould be miſtaken. The metonymy of *ſpecies* for the genus, by which we might be moſt eaſily miſled, is accordingly the moſt rare. This wiſe ſcope of nature would be utterly defeated, if, according to the notions of ſome lexicographers, and eſpecially of the Hebrew; languages were ſo conſtituted, that the principal ſignification ſhould point to the genus alone, and the others indicate only the ſpecies (*r*); for is there any thing which we are more apt to confound than the genus and ſpecies? This article of ambiguity I ſhall illuſtrate both by fictions and real facts.

Suppoſe that to two diſtempers eſſentially different, the ſame name has been given, on account of ſome external ſymptoms, common to both; the empyrics, and ſome phyſicians, no better than they, will treat them in the ſame manner, and thus inſtead of a remedy, we ſhall take poiſon (*s*).

(*r*) This miſtake I have confuted in the work already quoted, *Reflections on the Methods now uſed for underſtanding the ancient Hebrew language.*

(*s*) This misfortune, far from being imaginary, has really happened more than once, when, whether accidentally or fraudulently, the ſame name has been given to remedies and poiſons. Of this ſeveral inſtances occur in *Hill's Uſefulneſs of a Knowledge of Plants.*

Spat

Spat and Quartz are very easily diftinguifhable, but the miners in many places have only the firft name for both; and to this it is owing that they take thefe two minerals, which every day prefent themfelves to their eyes, for one and the fame, (though they abfolutely have nothing at all common, unlefs the tranfparency of a certain kind of fpat be reckoned fuch) and they themfelves are no farther acquainted with the inferior fpecies, than as facilitating or hindering the fufion of minerals.

Baron Wolf pretended to demonftrate the *principle of fufficient reafon*, by faying, that did any thing exift without fufficient reafon, it would follow that nihility muft be its fufficient reafon. M. de Premontval, member of that clafs of the academy, for which I particularly intend my work, has in laying open the infufficiency of this demonftration, clearly fhewn that it was founded only on the ambiguity of the word *nothing*, or *nonentity* (t).

The ancients have very much difputed on the fupreme or ultimate good. It was indeed the moft important queftion of their morality. We have feen what they meant by this *end of goods*, that is, a fcope, to which all other goods are only conducive means, being goods no farther than as leading to that end. Thus wealth is of itfelf no good. It only becomes fo, as enabling us to procure agreeable fenfations to ourfelves, and fecuring us from the fufferings of indigence, and an anxious folicitude for futurity. By *fupreme good*, is therefore to be underftood that identical good, the attainment of which is the capital object of my endeavours, making

French Tranflator's Remark.

(t) It is proper even to take notice that M. de Premontval having fhewn that the falfity of the demonftration becomes manifeft, on thinking, or on tranflating into French, whereas in the Latin and German expreffion, it remains ftrangely enveloped and intricate; and this it was which gave rife to the important queftion, on the influence of language on opinions, and of opinions on language. Never had the bulk of the German nation been mifled by the Wolfian philofophy, had not the two languages, which are moft familiar to them, the German and Latin, been more accomodated than the French, to the fophifm, on which the whole is founded. This, perhaps, is one of the moft remarkable paffages in the hiftory of the human mind.

use of the other goods, only as so many steps towards the attainment of it, and which without such intentions might be classed among things indifferent. It is not necessary that this be the greatest of all goods; whether great or small, it suffices that it is the object of my desires. But the Latin expression was ambiguous. *Summum bonum* may equally signify the greatest possible good; and the expression *supreme good*, in our modern languages, scarce admits of any other sense.

This ambiguity misled several philosophers, who not to stand neuter in discussions which had so much perplexed their predecessors, started that frivolous question, in what consists the *Supreme Good?* That is, in their opinion, the greatest of all goods. I call this question frivolous. Is it not possible, may not two or several goods be equal, and in this case who can warrant that there is one greater than all the other? Farther, may not a lesser good in a higher degree be equal to a greater good in a lesser degree, that we may be at a loss which to prefer? Is there then a geometry for goods and evils, and how are we to measure things, of which we know no common measure? But we will suppose that by the principle of *indiscernibles*, it was either impossible, or very improbable, that two beings shall reach the same point of felicity. The consequence will be, that there is but one only being which can enjoy the supreme good, and then all other goods are out of the question. This good was thought to be within every body's reach and conception, but can it ever be demonstrated that it is so? The supreme good, in reality, consists in being God; and to this, we neither can, nor are to pretend: several christian moralists, enamoured with the theological air of Plato's sentiments, hastily adopted them, but on a change of the question, they warped those doctrines from the meaning which that philosopher had annexed to them. They placed the supreme good in union with God: strange mistake! this moral union is not an individual good, it is a mean for acquiring a great quantity of goods to be eternally enjoyed, for attaining a felicity of interminable permanency, composed of numberless and infinitely diversified pleasures. It is not therefore what the question turns on, and much less is it what the ancient philosophers wrangled about. The subject of their altercations was, in effect, no more than to decide why, for inftance, a palatable difh, a fine profpect, riches, &c. are things which pleafe us. Would it not be abfurd to fay, that thofe things pleafe us, becaufe they procure us union with God? Should we like wine, becaufe it unites us with the Deity? Were this union the ultimate fcope to which all goods tend, the gratifications before mentioned, muft be ftricken out of the lift of goods, and be fet afide among things indifferent.

An expreffion of a later date, the ambiguity of which has not caufed lefs debate and confufion, is that of the *Law of Nature* (*u*). The learned and efpecially fuch as were not Civilians, framing to themfelves a law of nature, which, in the main, was nothing but morality, have thereby deprived themfelves of a whole fcience. Befides, morality, which by the divine fanction is changed into the *Law of Nature*, we clearly conceive a diftinct fcience, determining the rights which we reciprocally have over one another. Rights, which are valid, abftractedly from acknowledging the exiftence of a God, or without confidering him as legiflator. This fcience, on any difference arifing between nation and nation, becomes indifpenfible; as thefe differences cannot be brought to an iffue neither by morality nor the civil law; for what right have I to compel another to become virtuous, or to make war on a criminal people? Is it for me to chaftife them for their profligate difregard of duties? Grotius is the efteemable perfon to whom we owe the firft difcovery of this fcience; but it foon was in danger of being again confounded with morality. The Latin word for *right* is ambiguous, fignifying likewife *law*. Thus, for inftance, we fay the Roman right: and in this fenfe it is that moft divines confound right of nature with law of nature, that is, with morality, which is become a law by its connection with natural divinity, and they fly into a flame at hearing it faid of fome fins, that they are not contrary to the right of nature. This is what has partly given rife to the difputes in Germany, concerning M. Schmaus's *Right of Nature*. Though I by no means adopt all that learned perfon's principles, nor even

---

(*u*) Jufnaturæ.

would

would so much as vindicate the purity of his intentions, in certain Theses which apparently sap the very fundamentals of all morality; yet I am inclined to think that the outcry against that in which he denies the antiphysical sin to be repugnant to natural right, would not have been so loud had this right been better understood, for who will maintain that this sin warrants making war on a nation where it should prevail?

All these vehement disputes might have been prevented by a less equivocal term; but where is it to be found? That of *natural fitness* might be proposed (*x*), but whether the German expression answering to it would be approved, is a question.

I have said that the kind of homon; my including the genus and species under the same denomination had its dangers. This is the very case of a German word, equally signifying wonders and miracles. We give the name of *wonder* to all great events, all singular and unexcepted events which excite surprize and admiration (*y*); and herein custom happens to agree with etymology, but this appellation is more particularly appropriated to the immediate operations of divine omnipotence; it denotes miracles κατ' ἐξοχήν. This twofold meaning has led many divines to multiply miracles for God's greater glory, as they imagine, and to affirm that miracles are still performed in the kingdom of grace, though not perceived or taken notice of.

Instead of troubling the academy with the particulars of a controversy now actually on foot, I shall only say, that many of our old divines, who are quoted as authorities for the continuance of miracles, might in their use of that word understand it only in the sense annexed to it by Luther, when speaking of the works of nature, and especially of the rainbow, which in Latin answers to *Admirabilia Dei Opera*, the *wonderful works of God*.

(*x*) It is thus we render the German word *Befugniſſe* (jus ad Rem faciendam vel exigendam) though *fitneſs* be not precisely answerable to it, but the reader will by the context perceive how it is to be understood.

(*y*) Which in Latin may be termed *mirabilia*.

The vehement disputes among the Jews about the love of our neighbour are known to every body, and this dispute appeared to Jesus Christ of such concern, that he himself was pleased to illustrate and decide it: yet, in the main, it turned only on the ambiguity or double meaning of a Hebrew word *(z)*, and this word primarily signifies any man with whom I have something to transact, my neighbour, nay, my adversary, either in a law-suit or a duel; next it likewise signifies *a friend*. These divisions would never have been heard of had Moses written in German, and made use of that language in saying; *thou shalt love thy neighbour as thyself (a)*.

Accessary Ideas and Judgments.

Many are the objects for which some languages have no neutral terms, and which cannot be named without either praising or blaming them. Now if these accessary ideas are improper or erroneous, the judgment of the nations speaking those languages, will hardly escape being infected by those improprieties.

The meaning of the word *luxury* in French is very well known to all who understand that language. It is a word which neither prepossesses in favour of, or prejudices against the object denoted by it. Luxury, under certain limitations, is what sound policy will both approve and counnance, as without it no state can prosper and flourish. I would venture to undertake a justification of it, and bring many of my proofs from the holy scripture itself. But the German name for it is the question: that made use of by M. Justi *(b)*, is already charged with an accessary idea, which will necessarily expose it to the contempt and detestation of professors of morality, and especially ecclesiastics, or at least will withhold them from giving the due commendations to that discrete and al-

---

(z) רע.
(a) Neighbour may be rendered in German by *nehen-menfche*, as it were, *fellow-man*.
(b) Ueppigkeit, which may be rendered voluptuousness, or *libertinism*.

lowable

lowable luxury which I am speaking of. We have another word, which literally signifies superfluity *(c)*; and it is certain, the better only wants to be sufficiently received in this new signification. It is then strange that a thing for which we are yet without any neutral term, should be so exclaimed against, not only by preachers, but likewise by those who set up for oeconomists? And is not the language partly the cause of the ignorance of those people, who think they are wonderfully promoting the public good, in preaching up or recommending the most sordid parsimony.

Accessary ideas come especially under the notice of translators, by the difficulty of finding equivalent expressions in their language, whether they are to be accompanied with the same accessary ideas, or whether perfectly indifferent. Good translators often venture to amend this deficiency of the language by annexing to words new significations, with which the reader gradually becomes familiarized. The translation indeed may at first appear dark and loose. This is an inconveniency unavoidable, through the deficiency of the language, but it is compensated by a greater advantage.

I should scarce be excuseable, were I to omit the words, *time* and *space*, though I find nothing exceptionable in them. Whole schools of philosophers are known to look on time and space, only as *series* of monades mutations or phænomena, and admit no void either in one or the other; and these philosophers charge the language with misleading the imagination in this respect, by representing to it time and space, abstractedly from every other thing, and as essences subsisting of themselves. I do not well know what languages fall under this charge, and having not yet observed that any one is excepted, the censure perhaps may include them all. Let us take a short view of the German, the French, and the Latin.

I own that I do not see wherein either of those languages influences our judgments, or misleads our imagination. They do not so much as border on the question. They do not introduce the least accessary idea in the notions of *time* and *space*. Would such critics have these words, to draw

(c) Ueberfluß.

after

after them by way of regimen, a genitive fpecifying the things of which time and fpace are the comatentiona or feries? But that would be very fuperfluous, allowing even the truth of the thefis maintained by thofe philofophers. Every one knows there can be no order without things, and yet the word *order* may, in all languages, be ufed alone, and without regimen. Do they think that the very etymology of the terms fhould indicate time and fpace to be nothing more than fucceffions or feries? But this is the very thing in queftion; and did the language decide in their favour, the philofophers of a contrary opinion, might juftly accufe it of partiality. Is it not fomething out of the way to blame it for not favouring either one or the other party? And is it not ftill more out of the way to require from it, or rather to require from the people which forms it, and thefe are the multitude, generally illiterate, the decifion of one of the moft abftract queftions in all philofophy? If the geometrician be allowed to denote the line of which he is feeking the length by an arbitrary character, not in the leaft expreffive of any of the properties of that line; may not we likewife make ufe of the expreffions of a language, the etymology of which does not intimate to us any thing of the nature of the objects reprefented by thofe expreffions, or through time is become totally loft. The roots of the firft language muft certainly have been arbitrary figns; for from whence could they have been derived? And with what reafon can it be required that all the words of the modern languages fhould be real definitions and pictures of the objects?

Language, to be fure, accuftoms us to abftract time and fpace from the things which fill them, and that it fhould be otherwife is impoffible: without abftract ideas, what would become of metaphyfics? But if, farther, we can fo readily reprefent to ourfelves as void, time and fpace; this does not proceed from the language, but from the thing itfelf. Where is the impoffibility of a hollow fphere exifting, abfolutely filled with nothing; by fuppofing that there is no other univerfe, nor any thing without this fphere to comprefs it? What contradiction is there in this idea, that omnipotence could have created only this fphere, inftead of the world which it has made? But if the exiftence of fuch a fphere be poffible, that of a void fpace is likewife fo; the internal capacity of this fphere

being

being in reality an absolute void. This cannot be denied without denying this capacity any magnitude and extension, and thus the diameter and circumference would no longer have that reciprocal proportion, which the eternal laws of geometry require. Who will affirm that omnipotence cannot create a portion of insulated matter, separated from all other matter, and give it the form of a carpenter's square? And is it not evident by the determinate length of the hypothenuse, that there must be a void space between the two extremities of that square?

If our ready conception of a void space be owing to an error, this is not to be sought for in the language, but in our senses, to which, before we become acquainted with and have combined certain experiments, the whole expanse of the atmosphere appears a void space.

On the other hand, they who place eternity in a succession of instants, who conceive of it not as a mathematical point, but as an infinite line; these, I say, might with greater reason complain of the partiality of our language. According to them, eternity is only an infinite time, which we conceive by taking away from the time in which we exist, its beginning and end, and in this respect I am very much of their mind. Now the opposition in our language between time and eternity, in some measure contradicts this opinion, and favours school divinity, which excludes from eternity all succession, looking on it as an immense point, as a perpetual instant, and the whole of it present at once. I must, however, alledge in favour of the language, that in distinguishing time from eternity, nothing farther is meant by time than the continuance of life, or the duration of the world; and the expressions of *infinite time* (*d*), or *eternal time*, so far from being foreign to the idiom of our language, are perfectly suitable to it. The Latin word answering to eternity is *æternitas*, which is a contraction of *æviternitas*, of which *ævum* time, makes a part. Lastly, does not the church call eternity *secula seculorum*, *ages of ages*?

(*d*) *Oevum infinitum.*

Etymology

Etymology and Expreffions.

The inventors of new expreffions being no more infallible than the people who adopt them, the etymology of words, and compofed phrafes may as well perpetuate an error as a truth, and this error faftening on our mind in our tender years, will be the more contagious.

We all fee the dew lodged on the plants, but as we do not fee how it comes there, it would be quite as natural to compare it to perfpiration as to rain, and opinions would at leaft be divided were not the latter opinion fupported by long prejudice. The generality of people, and even the learned, who are not verfed in natural hiftory, both alike look on dew as vapours formed into drops falling from the fky. This however is a miftake which may eafily be cleared up, only by putting a receiver over the grafs in a dewy night *(e)*.

What furprifed me here is not that men have been miftaken; error is the lot of human nature; but it is the univerfality of this miftake, and the obftinate adherence to it, even after the truth of the matter has been fo manifeftly difcovered, that every one may convince himfelf of it with his own eyes. How comes it that there is but one opinion on this fubject, among all thofe who make no experiment and are unacquainted with phyfics, and this happens to be the wrong opinion? It is not our fenfes which deceive us, we fee drops, but there are drops of fweat as well as drops of rain. They who are abroad in the country all night, which is more often the cafe of the inferior clafs than men of letters, never per-

---

(*e*) An objection of a friend of mine makes it neceffary to explain myfelf more fully; I am far from denying that fogs iffuing from the earth do not leave drops on the trees through which they pafs; all I affirm is, that thefe drops do not defcend but rife from the earth and the plants; that the outfide of the receiver being a little wetted, is owing to thofe fogs. That dew afcends inftead of defcending is fufficiently evinced by the plants which had been covered being as wet, and even more fo, than thofe which remained in the open air: a ftill ftronger confirmation of it is, that they are no fooner uncovered than part of their dew flies off as a mift.

ceive any thing of this suppofed rain. Was there any thing more natural than to attribute to the drops on vegetables the fame origin as to thofe which proceed from our body? This humidity, when on glaffes and on ftones, was erroneoufly attributed to tranfpiration, and when the ftatues of the gods happened to be thus humectated, fuperftition cried out a portent! a prodigy! How came this moifture to be accounted an exudation where there was none, and no fuch thing to be thought of where it really is? I mean in the vegetables, the nature of which is much nearer a kin to us than that of glaffes and ftones. About day-break, when the dew, after having been very copious, is evaporating, countrymen and fhepherds fee fogs rifing and not falling. The German name for thefe mifts fhews their relation to dew *(f)*, and thus dew fhould rather be looked on as a gift from the earth than from the fky.

That this error has fpread fo very much is the fault of the languages in which it was at firft introduced. We have heard from our childhood *the dew of heaven, the dew falls*, as we have heard fay, *the ftone, the wall, the window gives*: Now it will be no eafy matter to reprefent to ourfelves as afcending what we have all our life been ufed to confider as falling, efpecially if we have made no enquiries on this head. I have ever found divines pertinacious in defending this miftake, and only becaufe they meet with thefe expreffions in fcripture; that is enough for them, juft as if the Hebrew people had never fpoke a word but what was infpired, or as if the prophets writing in that language, had not been obliged to make ufe of popular expreffions, they feem not aware that our naturalifts, though they know better, retain thofe expreffions to avoid the imputation of pedantry.

Here follows an inftance, precifely of the fame clafs. Manna bears a very near refemblance to dew; its origin is the very fame; the only difference being that it remains, whereas dew evaporates. From this reafon it is that in the countries, where manna is found, they have imagined that like dew, it fell from above, and this conceit has got footing in the languages. Both the Arabs and Hebrews fay with us, *that it comes from above*, or that it falls *(g)*. There is another kind which the Arabs, by way of

---

(f) Thauwolken, dew-clouds.
(g) ירד.

dif-

distinction, term *celestial manna (h)*. In the holy scripture we read that the manna fell along with the dew, and by the same figure which the profane poets make use of in calling the latter a gift of heaven, the truly inspired poet has called the manna *bread from heaven (i)*. These expressions, to which the orientals were accustomed from their early years, have confirmed them in the opinion that manna descended. It was not till the middle of the sixteenth century that the falsity of that opinion began to be seen into, and that in Italy manna was found to be no more than a gum exuding from plants, trees and bushes, on being pierced by certain insects. The expression, however, has been retained in the language, like those relating to dew and to the rising and setting of the sun, which I have before spoken of; it likewise occurs in Italian books, written long since the mistake was discovered *(k)*, and this shews that Moses might make use of the expression to the Israelites without countenancing the error to which the rise of it was owing. From the currency of the expression it is that this error still subsists among those who are not acquainted with the *materia medica*, that is among the generality; and as to the manna sent to the Israelites, though Moses's description exactly agrees with our modern manna, there are few divines who will suffer themselves to be undeceived.

The Jews in Jesus's time went still farther, making this error a handle to disparage the miracle of the multiplication of the loaves. *They said unto him, what sign shewest thou that we may see and believe thee? What doest thou produce? Our fathers did eat manna in the desert, as it is written he gave them bread from heaven to eat (l).* Nothing is more true in physics than the Saviour's answer, *Verily, verily, I say unto you that the bread which Moses gave you came not from heaven.* Now could, or would Christ have denied it, were the Hebrew phrase to be understood in its literal sense?

These wrong uses of the word *falling* put me in mind of those which *rising* occasions in occurrences of universal concern, and into which con-

(h) منّ السماء.
(i) Ps. LXVIII. 24.
(k) *Guida di forestieri* dell' Abatte Pompeo Sarrelli. Napoli. 1761. p. 594, dalle frondi si raccogli manna, che di notte dal celo si distilla come la rugiada (i. e.) from the leaves is gathered manna, which like dew, falls in the night from the sky.
(l) John vi. 30. 31.

sequently

sequently more enquiry and reflection might be expected. On the coining of bad money, for which, by a figure the Greeks themselves were unacquainted with, the names of crowns, groffchens, &c. are retained, it is evident that good money should be worth more of those kinds of crowns and groffchens, that is, it should be worth an agio or the difference of the standard.

It should then be said, such a coin, that of Bernburg for instance, *lowers in value*, the crown falls, it is worth less than before, and in the common course of things, it would usually be true to say that good money lowers with the bad, for if, by an allowance of 10 per cent, I receive for twenty pistoles, which make a hundred crowns, if I say I receive a hundred and ten crowns in bad money, the non value or deficiency of which is 50 per cent, it is very clear that the value of a pistole is extremely lowered to my detriment, as for a hundred crowns in gold I receive of fine silver, only the value of fifty-five crowns, and this from the stupidity of the people in looking no farther than the piece and inscription.

Whereas the pistole, the louis d'or, the good florin, &c. are said to rise, and except those who have philosophically investigated the substances of coins, or who have read what has been written about them within these ten years, and great traders, every body is misled by those expressions. They imagine a real augmentation or value when that is far from being the case. After laying out their capital in good coin, they fancy that the more monies lower, the better for them; and yet when bad money is again reduced to its real value, and the good is worth a difference of cent per cent, &c. which is the most favourable case, they are at most but where they were, they have preserved their capital, and that's all.

Nay, there are some who, after being so inconsiderate as to exchange a hundred in gold for fifty-five in silver, think they have been mighty cunning, and hug themselves for their address in the improvement of money. I have discussed this matter with persons of learning, and the difficulty in convincing them of so manifest a truth, shewed me how far this detrimental influence may go. When they were on yielding to the strength of my arguments, they were always withheld by a suspicion that perhaps it was only a mere verbal controversy, and whether, after all, to say, that the bad money lowers, or to say, that the good rises in value, was not tantamount. The objection, indeed, was specious, if the word *rising* is taken only relatively to bad coins, the upshot is the same, with only this difference, that for the justness of the relation, and to preclude any mistake, good coin should then be worth an agio of 50 per 100, and above. But it was understood in an absolute sense, and the good coins were looked on as an augmentation of wealth, and as an equivalent for a greater quantity of goods! A very great mistake!

If in an affair which may be strictly calculated, and which even, without calculation, seems as clear as the meridian sun; an affair, besides, of such public concern, I say, if in an affair of such a nature, the bulk of mankind are dazzled by an expression, which yet is not absolutely faulty; what will it be in abstract and metaphysical controversies, and what precautions are not required against the errors into which the impropriety of language may draw us? We are not, however, without preservatives against its snares; we may keep clear of them, both by doubt, which is the first precept of philosophy, and by frequently varying our modes of speaking. Away with that dry method, that superstitious adherence to the same expressions; it is infinitely more illusory and deceitful than that amiable philosophy, of which Plato has left us so charming a model, and which enlivens the most abstruse matters with the amenities of style, and the graces of poetry.

Etymology becomes a source of errors, not only when it is itself the offspring of error, but likewise when it causes figurative expressions to be taken for real definitions; or when, by length of time, expressions become so far changed as to convey a false etymology to the ear. This case indeed happens but seldom, and concerns only foreign words and phrases. When in fair weather a hovering cloud gradually extends itself over a certain hill in Switzerland, and this it seems is far from being uncommon, the hill looks as if it had a hat on; now this appearance gave rise to the name of *Mons Pileatus*, which afterwards was corruptively changed into *Mont de Pilate*, or *Pilate's Hill*; and that this false appellation might not

want

want an origin, the fable was invented of Pontius Pilate's throwing himself into a lake on such a mountain (*m*).

The other case is more frequent; it is incredible what a proneness there is in us to account whatever propositions we imagine to have discovered in etymology, infallible truths, as if the people, for it is they who make languages, could never be mistaken. It is very wrongfully, that only grammarians are accused of this fondness for etymology; there are many others not less infected with it, and full as ready to take for a proof a word of which they do not so much as know the inventor, and often will beat their brains to forge a specious proof, purely for upholding the authority of the word.

No two things are more alike than ice and chrystal, especially when split, and on this account it is, that in many countries the name of ice has been given to the latter. This, for instance was the primary meaning of the Greek word κρύςαλλος; and from this community of appellation, some have been for explaining the origin of chrystal: the most current opinion among the antients, was that chrystal is an ice which time has indurated, giving to its parts a fixedness and cohesion, by which they have totally lost their fluidity. I do not see how the sight could occasion this mistake, as, were it so, the like judgment must have been formed of *quartz*, of the transparent kind of *spath*, of the *selenites*, in a word, of all the diaphanous productions of nature. Etymology, therefore, may be reasonably apprehended to have caused the mistake, and indeed it is most frequently met with among the ancients, who laid a wonderful stress on Greek etymologies; and if some moderns are dazzled by them, I have observed that it is principally among the admirers of the Greek. Accordingly, it is only such, and not naturalists, that I shall briefly endeavour to convince of their mistake.

I. Chrystal is manifestly nothing but a kind of *quartz*, were it an indurated ice, the like must be said of all the other species of quartz, but such an absurdity, I believe, will scarce be maintained by any one, who

(*m*) For a full Description of Pilate's Hill, see the Hanover *Economical Chronicle*, 1758.

knows that great quantities of quartz are found in places where scarce any ice is to be expected, as in branches of mines, the air of which is always temperate, and must have been more inclinable to warmth, before the external air could make its way thither.

II. Chryſtal is diſtinguiſhed by a determinate form, that of an hexagonal obeliſk; a figure never found in pendant iſicles; theſe are rather roundiſh, without either point or angles, and too irregular to be any thing but accidental, and in which the coaleſcence of drops of water coming thither in divers directions is obvious to the ſight.

The German name of the Oolithos*(n)* equally tends to miſlead us. I very much queſtion whether the firſt inventor of that name took the ſtone for petrified roes of fiſh, and gave into an error ſo contrary to the nature of petrifactions, and diſproved by chymical experiments. It was unqueſtionably the outward reſemblance, which induced him, as it has induced many others to call ſhells from certain works of art, or of nature. It muſt then be the name, and only the names, heard all our life time but never rightly comprehended, which led thoſe who know there are petrifications, yet are not very well acquainted with their conſtituent parts, to confound with real roes of fiſhes, a lime ſtone mixed with coarſe ſand; and if it be ſuſpected that I am talking of an error merely chimerical, I can quote a memoir publiſhed at Rouſberg, the author of which carefully ſets down his predeceſſors in that error *(o)*. It is thus the man of learning is deceived, and in the ſame manner are the illiterate: Etymology miſleads them both. From this ſource, very probably, is derived the vulgar opinion, that the cancer may be cauſed by handling of putrified crabs.

Mr. Adamſon, in his Natural Hiſtory of Senegal, inveighs with no ſmall heat againſt theſe errors, and the etymological infatuation. He would have all the ſeveral productions of nature called by neutral names, and without any derivation; they ſhould be mere arbitrary ſigns, of no

---

(*n*) *Regen-Stein.* Stone conſiſting of fiſhes rows.

(*o*) Quaſ:io naturalis Pruſſica de Oolitho Regiomontano, 1733, by Charles Henry Rappott.

farther import, and quite irrelative to other things *(1)*. This remedy seems to me worse than the disease; if etymologies have their falsities, they on the other hand, intimate to us many truths, which otherwise we should never discover, or at least not till very late, and are truths to be rejected, because they are intermixed with error? Nearly the like mixture is met with in all libraries, are they therefore to be destroyed. Farther, etymologies are a great help to memory, which certainly stands in need of help amidst the abstruse investigations of natural history, on the other hand, new words, without derivation, would convey sounds too uncouth for our ears readily to take in, which would be laying memory on the rack. It is, therefore, my opinion, that we should be sufficiently guarded against mistakes, would the votaries of physical sciences carefully bear in mind these two things *(p)*: 1*st*, That most etymologies, being figurative expressions, are not intended to express the nature of objects. 2*d*, That even when this is the intention of them, they are no more than the thoughts of an anonymous individual, and which, of course, require the same examination as all the thoughts we meet with in the course of our reading.

But I will suppose these two rules not to be a sufficient security to the naturalist against every possible error, what expedient remains then for the

(p) His words are; "Experience teaches us that most of the significative names, which have been given to objects of natural history, are become improper and false, as new properties, or properties contrary to those which gave rise to these names, are discovered, therefore to guard against contradictions, figurative terms are to be exploded, and such only used as cannot be referred to any etymology whatever, that they who are infatuated with etymologies, may not be led to annex false ideas to words." In this the author requires an impossibility: what signifies inventing new sounds? the people will soon alter them to an affinity with some national sounds and common words, as among innumerable other instances, the Germans of *Muslimin*, have made *Muselman*. The execution of Mr. Adamson's scheme would become a very copious source of errors, like that of Pilate's Mountain above mentioned. He goes on in this manner.

(q) "Names should be like blows, or Games of Chance, between which there is generally no connection: the less significative, the less relation they have to other names or known things, the better, because the idea being fixed to one single object, would comprehend it much more distinctly, than when blended with other objects in affinity to it."

meta-

metaphyſician, and the learned in other branches? Muſt they alſo invent barbarous languages, the words of which are to have no manner of connection or analogy between them? A ſad ſtroke to the ſciences! The moſt that a perſon could learn would be one, and that but very deficiently; like the Chineſe we ſhould waſte our life in retaining thouſands of characters, and what is worſe, be farther like them in this, that, after all our toil, we ſhould have learned no more than what others knew; and to carry any one ſcience to its perfection, would be utterly impoſſible. Mr. Adamſon ſeems to have had a thorough knowledge of every circumſtance relating to Senegal; but he is not acquainted with the nature of language.

In my laſt ſection I ſhall make ſome remarks, by which a true eſtimate may be formed of his project. It is with phraſes as with the etymologies of words: they were true in their origin, where their ſenſe was only figurative, but being afterwards explained in their proper ſenſe, they are become ſources of errors to whole nations, and of errors to which thouſands of years may not put a period.

They, who hold every thing to depend on providence, without any allowance to a chance, which it could not foreſee, or to a neceſſity which it could not withſtand; in a word, the ſticklers for the doctrine of the beſt world, may attribute to God all the good and evil that falls out, as the reaſon of its exiſtence lies in thoſe ſcenes of the world which preceded it, and the primordial reaſon of the whole from the firſt univerſal arrangement, of which God has foreſeen all the conſequences. This good and this evil are only a mediate, and not an immediate effect of omnipotence, which executed, a plan from whence, by a long chain of conſequences, they were to reſult: Moral good and moral evil, are here in the like caſe, though it is the former which has been the ſcope of the diſpoſition; and the ſecond has been admitted only becauſe the excluſion of it would have diſconcerted the plan, and rendered it leſs good than it is.

The Orientals, to indicate this arrangement, made uſe of bold figures; much leſs common among us, though not totally unknown.

The

The people of Berlin fay that all marfhal Daun did in his laft invafion of Saxony in 1758, was the burning the fuburbs of Drefden. Herein they fpeak of the mediate caufe, without faying that it is only mediate, and ufe the very expreffion which denotes the immediate caufe. In the eaft they go ftill far greater lengths. There God *has done and commanded* all that men do, however, contrary to his commandments. Shimei breaks forth into imprecations againft David; from that time God has ordered Shimei to *curfe David*. The people after all Ifaiah's difcourfes and exhortations are little affected by them, as being what they had long been ufed to; then it is, God has faid to the prophet, *harden thou the hearts of this people;* and no mention is made of the innocent means which happened to be productive of this obduracy. Miracles, by being multiplied, do not convince Pharoah; they make no impreffion on his mind; and it was God by whom thefe miracles were wrought; this the Hebrew phrafeology terms *God has hardened Pharaoh's heart.* The Ifraelites fuffer themfelves to be deceived by lying prophets, feeding them with illufive hopes of happier times. Here again it is; God has deceived them. If we collect together all the like paffages in the fame point of view, it will be palpably manifeft that an immediate operation of God on the will and underftanding is not, cannot be, the import of them; but that they relate only to the natural and common operations of providence *(r)*.

When evil actions are the queftion, thefe ways of fpeaking aftonifh us, and this very aftonifhment fhould give us to know that thefe expreffions are figurative. This is lefs manifeft, when morally good actions, as converfion, faith, holinefs, and fanctification are attributed to the deity.

By the too frequent ufes of this figure, it comes gradually to be no longer taken for a figure; and a literal fenfe is annexed to it. God is imagined to be the immediate caufe of all the actions attributed to him. He miraculoufly produces what moral good and evil is in man, or, at

---

(r) Exod. iv. 28. ix. 12, 16. Deut. iv. 19. xviii. 14. xxix. 25. 2 Sam. xvi. 10. xxiv. 1. Jerem. iv. 10. Eccl. xiv. 9. xx. 25.

least, the latter, by with-holding a miraculous grace, without which we cannot abstain from the commission of sin. According to this opinion, God discomposes the course of events; he never chooses a thing as naturally resulting from what precedes it because the order in which it comes is the best of all. No, on the contrary, it is by an absolute decree that he makes choice of it; then considers and finds out means for bringing it to effect; and when these means are not in the common course of nature, he by his immediate influence alters that course.

This is what happened to Mahomet, whose ignorance could not enter into a philosophic examination of his language, and distinguish letter from figure. The Arabic, which has a very near affinity with the Hebrew, and which speaks of the works of providence *with the like emphasis*, induced the prophet, who was of a strong and saturnine fancy, and he himself an odd medley of the impostor and enthusiast, to teach the absoluteness of the divine decrees in the most rigorous sense; and make man a mere machine. It will appear, that there is all the reason in the world to charge his error on his language, when we consider the many mistakes it has led him into. For instance, on what account could he forbid killing locusts, had he not looked on them to be *God's army*; and his looking on them as such, was because such is the meaning of the Arab word for locusts (s). The same language often describes sin under the figure of a load or burden (t) of which a man cannot rid himself. This Mahomet understood of a material burden; and, accordingly, maintained, that the damned carried their crimes on their back, and especially all the goods they had stolen; and this error he introduced into the Alcoran, on account of a cloak having been stolen out of the booty; and some sons of Belial had the effrontery to suspect that the thief was no other than the prophet himself.

A like doctrine, relating to an absolute decree, and its immediate effects in the conversion or hardening of men has spread itself in Christianity;

(s) جنود الله *Gunud' Allahi.*
(t) ذنب

a doctrine

a doctrine which has met with champions and antagonists in the three several Christian religions; and it may be questioned, whether it does not proceed from the same source as above. Thus much is certain, that the continuance of it is owing to a false and perverted explanation of some bibliacal phrases; taking eastern figures in the most strict literal meaning: still this is not the whole of what I mean. St. Austin is incontestibly the patriarch of this doctrine among the Christians. With a slender portion of learning he had a very warm imagination; he was an African, and by language a Carthaginian. Latin indeed was spoken in the cities of Africa, but it was not the Roman Latin, being adulterated with a strong African tinge. If Latin was the body of that language, its soul was formed of the Punic, St. Augustine's mother-tongue, and he was so well versed in it, as sometimes to make use of it for better illustrating Hebrew phrases (*u*). Thus the good bishop spoke Hebrew without knowing it. Had he been acquainted with the Hebrew alphabet, and taken some little pains in studying the difference between that language and the Punic language of that time, instead of being reproached as scandalously ignorant of both the original languages of the holy scripture, he would have been honoured as the father of oriental philology.

Let us, but without injuring St. Austin's reputation, by stretching the comparison too far, compare the two doctors of absolute decrees. The imagination of both was strong, and bordering on enthusiasm. They both had a natural bent to poetry; though, in St. Augustine, grace afterwards converted this bent into declared aversion. Neither of the two had so much learning as to guard themselves from the elusions of figurative stile; one was an Arab, and the other a Hebrew. Would it be any egregious mistake to charge part of the origin of an error of so long a standing, and which has spread itself among the three branches of Christianism, on those languages? I say in part; it being known that St. Augustine was farther misled by a kind of *spiritual experience*; on which he relied without any sufficient examination of it.

(*u*) Gen. xxx. 30.

SECT. VI.

Arbitrary Beauties.

OF all the antient languages which have reached our times, the Greek is perhaps the fittest for furnishing us with instances of errors; the origin of which was solely owing to arbitrary beauties; but under the sanction of time and custom, they became laws; from which they who spoke or wrote in that language could not safely deviate. The voice of the people determined propriety and beauty without taking into consideration the advantage or detriment which might result from the diction. These beauties were pretty much like those of the Gothic architecture; but he who writes for a nation must conform to its caprices.

Extreme fondness for harmony, and an extreme aversion against rude sounds, may introduce errors into history. Now this nicety the Greek language particularly affected. Herodotus excuses himself more than once, when under a necessity of inserting proper names with a foreign sound; and some he chooses rather to omit. My Teutonic ear, indeed, is proof against these kinds of cacophonies; but very certain it is, that Grecian ears were extremely offended at them. The consequences of this delicacy were two-fold.

Either foreign proper names were changed till they became more musical, that is, till they became Grecian, and seemed derived from a Greek root: the baneful source of innumerable errors!

Would not children and the commonality naturally imagine that the nations, the names of whose towns and rivers were Greek, had originally spoken the Greek tongue. This false opinion carrying with it an air of patriotism, was too pleasing not to be obstinately defended by the multitude of the learned. It is the weakness of us all that we are for making every other nation a colony of ours. I am not here speaking of the fables to which these kinds of etymologies give birth, like that of *Pilate*'s *Mountain* before-mentioned.

Or these proper names were translated; and this was the way of the Greeks with the Egyptian towns; but a way which throws history into great confusion and uncertainty; or, at least, makes the study of it extremely difficult: and historical, geographical, and other such dictionaries, which, without an universal knowledge, are indispensibly necessary to a scholar, become quite useless.

The Hebrew language has in this last respect either a great advantage, or a great fault, writing all foreign names so as to appear Hebrew, or, at least, reducible to four radical letters. Let us only call to mind the Egyptian names which are in the bible; at the same time not forgetting that their original the Egyptian and the Hebrew languages, have absolutely nothing in common; but these names being Hebrewized, nothing is easier than to find out Hebrew etymologies for them; and it is this easiness which has indicated such etymologies in all foreign proper names. Among other great men, Bochart himself has not escaped the delusion; it is, as it were, the reigning *influenza* in all who make Hebrew their principal study. The Arabic does not allow itself in such extravagant alterations: all foreign names in it remain within knowledge; and this contempt of false delicacy gives its geographers and historians a great preference. It was certainly in its victorious marches through so many nations varying in speech, that this language contracted its masculine roughness.

Such was the passion or infatuation of the Greeks for eloquence, that, in conformity to it, their historians were obliged to put formal speeches in the mouths of all their principal characters; and in contempt of the plainest laws of probability, to give an oratorial turn to their whole conversation. Josephus the historian owns that he knew no more of the history of the ancient Jews, than what he had read in the old testament, but setting up for atticism, and desirous of being read in Greece, it behoved him of course to make the prevailing taste his rule of composition; and very closely does he keep to it. Where the original text scarce exceeds a line,

line, he embroiders it with long declamations; and where the text, though more ample, contains only plain and natural expreſſions, he ſubſtitutes the flowers of rhetoric, and fictitious embelliſhments. Compare the ſpeech which he puts in the mouth of Judah, when ſpeaking to Joſeph (x), with that which, according to Moſes's narrative, Judah in reality made on that occaſion (y): the latter is full of affectionate ſentiments, and natural firmneſs; the other is languid, and bear culpable marks of art. In a word, there being no poſſibility that Judah had leiſure to form ſuch a ſtudied ſpeech before-hand, it is one of the moſt impertinent fictions with which a writer can impoſe on his reader, and try his patience or ſtupidity. This I ſay, not as blaming Joſephus, he could not do otherwiſe: his reputation as a writer depended on ſuch decorations: had he kept to truth and nature, his book would have been deſpiſed by the literati and polite.

Into what miſtakes is he led by forming his idea of an hiſtorical fact from theſe fictions? and ſtill more frequently do they disfigure, under a falſe parade, thoſe cloſe, natural, and pictureſque expreſſions, which ſo ſtrongly ſet forth the ſentiments of heroes, and are, as it were, animated effigies of them. How uncertain muſt hiſtory be, when the hiſtorian is, by the genius of his language, forced to diſguiſe truth with fictitious additions. It would be rather better for theſe oſtentatious decorations to be put in verſe; as do the Arabs ſometimes: for who, but one utterly void of reaſon, can imagine, that a hero, amidſt the thunder of war, and the diſtractions of a battle, could have compoſed and repeated a long ſtring of verſes; and that theſe were exactly retained in memory verbatim by all about him. Such madmen are ſeldom met with, and only among ſcholars.

Our modern languages have ſhaken off this kind of pedantiſm, but retaining other defects and whims not a whit better. The French language appears to me more fond of theſe falſe ornaments than any other;

(x) Antiq. II. 6.
(y) Gen. xliv.

and especially affecting a mighty predilection for words, and what is called wit. Their very classical authors slip into this fault; which is never more striking than on comparing them with the beautiful simplicity of English writers, who seem to mind only things. This remark on the French, cannot reasonably incur their displeasure: Do not they themselves boast of being like the Greeks? And indeed the speeches among the Greeks, and the French characters or *portraits* wear a very irrational parade of eloquence. Truth often suffers by these embellishments. If they set off dramatic pieces, in history they are faulty to the last degree; especially as little care is taken to draw from nature, the whole study being to charge these portraits with striking features.

Another beauty of the French stile consists in bold thoughts, propositions without either proof or restriction, and advanced with an air of over-bearing superiority, as if unquestionable; and which please by being singular and unexpected; and that affected brevity which is dignified with the appellation of an energetic precifeness. That this stile is extremely detrimental to historical and philosophical truths, is self-evident; this, however, may be only the fault of fashionable writers, without having yet eaten into the substance of the French language. Some of the best writers are intirely clear of this defect; and did I not apprehend being suspected of adulation towards the academy, I could name them. But should this fashion go on half a century more, every one who writes in French will be obliged to conform to it.

SECT.

SECT. VII.

Reflections on the preceding Articles.

I Conclude with three remarks.

1. The greater part of the errors do not proceed immediately from the language; but they are retained and perpetuated by expressions originally pregnant with them.

2. All known languages may have certain common errors; and to some of which nature does not lead us. Of this we have seen instances in the fall of dew and manna; and other expressions not indeed erroneous, but absolutely arbitrary, still more manifestly evince the affinity of different languages. For instance, it is very arbitrarily that we Germans give the name of (z) *wisdom's teeth* to those which come after the twentieth year. Now the Arabs are found to use the same term (a); and they call a *wise man* one who has these teeth (b). Among the Greeks, Hippocrates makes use of the like expression (c); and yet those three languages are totally different. There is, as to manner of expression, an affinity between all the several languages of Europe, which does not proceed from any connection or intercourse between the several nations; but from the Latin tongue, as the idiom of the learned, and of the church. It is that which we have taken for our model; and it being the first which we learned by rules, the grammars of the other languages have all, more or less, availed themselves of it. The learned partly think in Latin, and what they compose in their mother-tongue, is often no more than translations of Latin thoughts. The primitive preachers from whom our forefathers received the truths of Christianity, had them engraven on their minds in Latin. The Latin is not only the daughter of the Greek, but when grown up, it affected all its mother's ways, and particularly to express herself with elegance.

(z) *Weisheits-Zæhne.*
(a) اضراس العقل .
(b) منجذ .
(c) σωφρονιςηρες Hipp. περι σαρκων. c. 14. 3.

In the moſt antient Greek authors we meet with manifeſt traces of a connection with the Hebrew *(d)* ; a connection which indeed does not relate to etymology, but it relates to the way of thinking. It may poſſibly come from the Phœnicians, to whom the genius of the Greeks owes its firſt cultivation ; or from the Egyptian hieroglyphics,. a ſource with which both the Greek and Hebrew poets have been equally buſy. The former make no difficulty of owning the theft, and as to the latter, a probable conjecture of it may be founded on their long continuance in Egypt; and this probability is ſo far ſtrengthened by the great number of hieroglyphical paſſages, with which their writings are interſperſed *(e)*.

Laſtly. The Saracens, over-running Europe, were the inſtruments of inſinuating into the palpable darkneſs of thoſe ages a glimmering of ſcience which, faint as it was, produced a new alloy of the European languages with the oriental.

From thence it is, that all theſe languages are ſo much alike in the turn of thought, as to give cauſe of ſuſpicion that they have certain errors in common ; and to avoid theſe errors will be a matter of great difficulty, unleſs, as in the caſe of manna and dew, they are diſcovered to us by the ſenſes or experience. I am not indeed acquainted with any ſuch error: were I, it would no longer be an error to me, and I ſhould have made a diſcovery which has eſcaped all thoſe nations ; but that is far beyond both my abilities and expectations; and ſuch diſcoveries, poſſibly, are neither very neceſſary, nor of any great importance. I could however wiſh that ſome philoſophical genius, who, beſides being conſummately verſed in our languages, was equally maſter of ſome remote language, as the Chineſe, or one of the American languages, would ſet down to an examination of this point.

(d) See M. Erneſti's work *de veſtigiis linguæ Hebraïcæ* in lingua Græca.
(e) See the diſſertation on the mythology of the Hebrews, which the author has added to a work of M. Lowth (now biſhop of Oxford) intitled, *Prælectiones de ſacra poeſi Hebræorum, cum notis et epimetris. Jav. Dav. Michaelis*, p. 181—204. of the Gottingen edition.

L   It

(3.) The republic of letters, as confifting of fo many different nations, ftands in need of a literary language; and the faults of this language may be very detrimental to literature.

It is not from choice, but merely from cafualty, that the Latin has attained to this dignity; and it partly owes it to religion. I look on it as a happy circumftance that it is a dead language; the living are fo liable to variations, that books at the end of two centuries, if not, become, in a great meafure, unintelligible, at leaft, are never read with the original guft. Not that the Latin is without many inconveniencies; and one very interefting is the want of terms in natural hiftory, that Linnæus, and others, have found themfelves under a neceffity of forgeing a barbarous Latin, of which Cicero would not have underftood a fingle word; and which even thofe among ourfelves, who in the current Latin are not to feek, are obliged to ftudy as attentively as idioms totally unknown are ftudied.

I do not fee that this way can remedy the inconveniencies of which I have been fpeaking; or I rather fear, that the evil does not admit of a remedy; every nation by intermixing its language will make a barbarous Latin for itfelf, and thus unintelligible to others. This fhould be a leading motive with the learned to apply themfelves to the purity of the antient Latin.

I could much rather have wifhed that chance had conferred this preeminence on the Greek; efpecially when I confider that the Latin itfelf cannot do without it; and that it is obliged to borrow from it moft of its medical and phyfiological terms, which thus are quite obfcure to all who are not converfant with the Greek. The verfatility of this language, and the infinite diverfity of compounds which it admits of, would have been advantages not to be met with in any other. This feveral perfons of the higheft eminence in learning have perceived, but too late the die was caft before any choice could be made, and we are carried away by its decifion.

The Eaft, which owes the univerfality of the Arabic language to its falfe religion, may have the advantage of us from the infinite richnefs of

that

that language. It is a fource to which we ourfelves have frequent recourfe, for expreffing the productions of nature. Befides, it is nearly as invariable as if it were a dead language. But thefe advantages are totally loft in it. The Mahometan is in no need of a learned language, as little concerning himfelf about learning.

SECT. IV.

Remedies againft the noxious Influence of a Language.

All I have to fay in this fection is reducible to four articles. To avoid the errors arifing from the language; to retain what ufeful things are in it; to correct its faults; and laftly to examine the fcheme of a new learned lguage, properly fo called. Having in the preceding fections tranfitorily touched on moft of the fubjects relative to thefe articles, the formal difcuffion of them here may be abridged.

ARTICLE I.

Precautions for avoiding Errors, into which the Language leads.

Here I need only repeat the rules intimated in the foregoing fection.
1. Credit no propofition purely becaufe the etymology implies it, or feems to imply it. Etymology is the voice of the people; which the philofopher always fufpects, yet always attends to it.
2. Vary your expreffions; abftain from the jejune method; and endeavour to blend a variegated ftile with folidity of thought.

When there are several ways of expressing the same thing, it is scarce possible that the error which has insinuated itself into one; should have crept into all the other. These kinds of errors are not systematical. We have seen how the common magazine of a language has come to be filled. One has introduced such an opinion, another the contrary opinion. Wit, at first, taken only for wit, jocularity, love of novelty and singularity, are found to have concurred in the accumulation; and often, when error is become the universal opinion, a new expression, at first looked upon only as a beautiful figure, has restored truth.

Languages, in a great measure, consist of poetical expressions; which, by a long and frequent imitation of them in prose, are become prosaic. Poets being obliged to strike out of the common road, and study figures, their enthusiasm often suggests to them the most singular comparisons, such as do not lie on the surface of the mind. Thus it is very probable, that for all the erroneous expressions the poetic stile furnishes an antidote. Not that the poets have discovered truth; but, in the quest of new similitudes, they have hit on it without knowing it. Though the error of dew and manna falling from the sky be general, yet is there a kind of manna, or, to speak more properly, a wild honey, generated in trees, with only a degree of fluidity more, of which Virgil has said,

Et duræ quercus sudabunt roscida mella.

Therefore, if I have above intimated that certain errors had got such deep root in all known languages, that it was to be feared it would be impossible to discover and extirpate them; I shall here offer some preservatives, which may, in a good measure, encourage us against such despondency.

The noxious influences of a language, but little affect the man of true learning. Generally speaking, they are such only to the ignorant; to persons of a superficial knowledge; to the learned of a contracted genius: in a word, to those who are obstinately tenacious of the same expressions; or to those whose whole erudition lies in languages. And the

best

best of it is, that on the sources of these errors being known to us, we are able to guard against them, as against all other prejudices. The academy therefore could not make use of a more proper way for obviating the pernicious influence of language, than by proposing an enumeration of them for a prize problem.

I cannot, I own, conceive that any of the concurring pieces will throw a sufficient light on this subject, not excepting even that which the academy shall crown; accounting it the least imperfect. Essays are all that can be expected; and let me here be permitted to excuse the imperfection of that which I have the honour of offering to the academy.

The subject is both new, and little canvassed; the few strictures on it (found scattered in the writings of some great men) amount to no more than faint glimmerings.

To satisfy the academy, will require a philosophical genius, and a sagacity capable of penetrating into all the mazes of human errors; and with these must be joined a vast knowledge of languages. Such a writer must be able to compare the languages of the most distant nations, and between which and ours there is nothing of that relation which, as I have said, subsists between all the European, and those which go by the name of Oriental languages. The Chinese language, for instance, together with all its etymological erudition, must be as familiar to him as his own language; besides an equal acquaintance with the Oriental languages, properly so called, and those of Europe; and this will not be all; he must farther be deeply versed in the history of the opinions of all those nations. The academy is certainly too equitable to require a compleat deduction, to which nothing under such a various accumulation of knowledge, is adequate; its indulgence will be satisfied with a good essay; and such an essay will infinitely contribute to enlarge and concentrate the empire of truth, now divided among different philosophers, consummately acquainted with different foreign languages; it may serve them as a plan for digesting their collections, and a clew to guide them in their investigations. What a happiness would it be, were the academy itself, either by new prizes, or by its authority, to continue encouraging the

the labours of philosophers, and digesting the discoveries made on this head in all the parts of the universe, thus making itself the repository of so valuable a treasure.

Languages, generally speaking, would deserve that philosophy should devote a particular science to them; but let not this science, by any means, be reduced into a system, till experience had collected and arranged every particular of it. The academy appears to have had the foundation of it in its eye; and probably the glory of enriching the republic of letters with such a science, will be another jewel in its crown, already so resplendent. I could very much wish that it may one day think fit to bestow its attention and encouragement on the following question: *How can language be introduced among men, who as yet have no language, and by what means may it attain among them to the perfection in which we see it?*

This question has a great influence on that which I am now discussing, but I have foreborne touching on it, to avoid bewildering myself in the vastness of its extent.

3. Such of the learned who are fundamentally versed in the foreign languages, are, on that account, more guarded against the delusions of their mother tongues, having, as it were, several mother tongues, which they can compare and correct one by the other.

ARTICLE II.

Preservation of what is useful in Language.

Languages retain the riches they have acquired, when the sciences flourish in those nations where they are spoken; when they are used in matters of science, and when good writers, studious of preserving the purity of their language, never make use of foreign terms but on a very great exigency, as where their own language does not afford any so expressive.

expreſſive. Wherever this is not the caſe, the national language falls to decay, and with it the ſciences. This ſhews that the ſcrupulous attention which many learned men are pleaſed to call frivolous, and almoſt account a grammatical pedantry, ſo far from deſerving that treatment, is a point of very great importance to human knowledge.

I am not acquainted with any preſervative againſt the danger which, as we have ſeen, threatens etymology. The lot of mortality is what all mortal things muſt undergo. However, if there be words, the etymology of which, with length of time, wears out of knowledge, it is to be hoped, that language will replace them with others equally uſeful for the like purpoſe.

ARTICLE III.

Improvement of the Language.

What I have ſaid in the ſecond ſection on the method for augmenting the richneſs of a language, is the beſt advice I can offer here, and its uſefulneſs may be further extended to other branches of our knowledge. The beſt remedy againſt equivocations and ambiguities, and prepoſſeſſions ariſing from acceſſory ideas, is to enrich the language with expreſſions, which admit of no equivocations, and clear of all acceſſory meaning.

There is no need of extirpating erroneous etymologies, for reality is never to be inferred from etymology. In making uſe of a word or a phraſe, ſprung from a falſe opinion, I do not therefore adopt that opinion, and if I know the real truth of the matter, I am not under an error. I may make uſe of an expreſſion, though it be a wrong deſcription, or definition, I ſay I may uſe it as a figure or an image. If a poet speaking of a pilot who is loſing ſight of Italy, may ſay, *Italy ſets*, or *Italy ſinks*;

sinks into the sea.. The Copernician, may without any trespass against astronomy, say *the sun sets*, or *the sun sinks into the ocean*.

I rather believe the scholar to be in some measure obliged to regulate himself herein, as every individual in the empire of language. It is not for him to give laws nor proscribe established expressions: if he takes so much on him he is ridiculed, and deservedly; it is no more than a just mortification to his ambition, and the penalty of his usurping on the rights of the people. Language is a democratical state, where all the learning in the world does not warrant a citizen to supersede a received custom, till he has convinced the whole nation that this custom is a mistake; and if he substitutes a new term in lieu of that which has always been used to indicate a certain object, how can he expect to be understood? The German word for a *crayon* is a compound of two words, one of which signifies lead *(f)*; you insist that it should be altered to iron *(g)*, the substance of the *crayon* being feruginous: but do you think that for your say-so the current name must be altered, or that your corrections will be minded? The crayon is like lead in its colour and softness, and that justifies the appellation. Besides the whole nation is not informed of the mistake, and the commonalty have other things to mind than to sift philological mistakes; which farther cannot be done without a knowledge of all the sciences in their whole compass. On the other hand, scholars are not so infallible that every thing is to be referred to them. Were they allowed a decisory power, the errors of language, I am sure, instead of diminishing, would be continually increasing. Learned heads teem with them no less than the vulgar; and the former are much more imperious, that we should be compelled to defer to their innovations, and implicitly to receive every false opinion of theirs.

This consideration, doubtless, has been overlooked by some divines; who, from a notion that no expression arising from an error, can have found place in the sacred scripture, imagine that all the words in the

---

(*f*) *Bley-stift*, } The French say *Mine de plomb*, i. e. black lead. It would be ridicu-
(*g*) *Eisen-stift*, } lous to go about changing it to *Mine de fer*, black iron.

bible,

bible, and taken in the moſt literal ſenſe, is always *phyſically* true. I have vindicated the bible which they injure; and this I ſhould not have taken on me, as a needleſs work, had we not recently ſeen ſome new Hermeneutics brand, as deiſtical, this poſition: that the ſcripture conforms its phraſeology to popular cuſtom.

Erroneous etymologies may, however, be in ſome meaſure rectified, by aſſociating with them more preciſe and exact expreſſions to be invented for the ſame objects. This is a right inveſted in every one who is maſter of the language he ſpeaks: he may form new words, and form new phraſes, provided they coincide with the genius of the language, and be not over multiplied. If theſe expreſſions come to obtain the ſame vogue as the erroneous expreſſions, we are in them provided with a counterpoiſon; at leaſt, language does no longer draw us into error neceſſarily: they ſometimes, in the hands of ſkilful writers, ſhall riſe on the ruins of the falſe expreſſions, which, ever after, ſhall no more be heard, or only from the mouths of the populace.

As for Gothic ornaments, I know but two ways of exterminating them: more perfect models and ſatyr. In a democracy where the law is not ſufficient to bring men to reaſon, ridicule muſt be called in to its aſſiſtance.

I have intimated ſome amendments which ſhould be made in language; but who ſhall undertake them, and in what method are they to be conducted? Not by any act of private authority; that would be a flagrant infringement on the rights of language, which are democratical; beſides the general deriſion of ſuch arrogance. It is not for thoſe ſcholars, whoſe whole merit conſiſts in erudition, to take theſe amendments in hand; ſuch an enterprize requires perſons capable of taking the lead and gaining imitation. In ſhort, it is a taſk for claſſical authors alone; and all theſe are not qualified for it: they muſt be original geniuſes, eminent in their claſs, reſpected even by thoſe learned men who value things only, and ſuch maſters of their language, as to be the acknowledged ſtandards of its purity and elegance. Theſe are the writers who may give new meanings to old expreſſions, whilſt they do not abuſe the public indulgence, by loading the language with too great a multiplicity of innovations;

and these their privileges are of very antient date: thus Cicero familiarized the Latin to expressions the import of which, before his time, could scarce be so much as thought but in Greek only *(b)*. These writers often rise to such vogue, that to deviate from the stile which they have introduced, is enough for an expression to be accounted faulty.

No person can assume to himself the authority of a classical author: and to give any room for being suspected of entertaining such a claim, would itself be an unpardonable presumption; yet is every reformer of sciences to cultivate his language with as much application as if he really aimed at that distinction. Here it is that divine poetry triumphs most signally: blending itself with the serious sciences, it imparts to them a new degree of perfection. The time which an intercourse with the muses steals from those extraordinary persons who are both great poets and great scholars, is so far from being lost, that an infinite advantage accrues from it to the national knowledge; and the rewards bestowed on those favourites of Apollo meet with ample returns. It is evident, at first sight, that I do not here mean those versifiers whose talent reaches no farther than the art of making verses; nor even those scholars, however eminent, who force their genius, and will rhyme in spite of the *nymphs of Pindus*. They never rise above mediocrity, and the language is not affected by their influence.

Lastly, good translations as requiring labour, deserve a suitable rank among the means of improving a language. They bring to light the faults and deficiencies of the language, and remedy them by new expressions; but the translator must, in some degree, be possessed of the genius and talents of a classic author; he must be at least faithful, must thoroughly comprehend the meaning of the original, and his very translation should have an original appearance. It was translating and imitating the Greek, that brought the Latin to be what it is. Even in Cicero's time, it was still a question whether philosophy could be treated of in Latin. Nothing would more contribute to the perfecting of our lan-

---

(b) De Nat. Deorum. 1. §. 8. 8.

guages than beautiful tranflations of the immortal productions of ancient Greece and Rome. But I could wifh them to be both lefs fcholaftic than thofe which come out in Germany, and more clofe than thofe of France. The German is unqueftionably a great gainer by tranflations. It is tranflations which have fitted it for being ufed in the fciences, and which have enriched it with the turns of moft of the other living languages. But bad tranflations have done us little lefs harm. Our Mecenafes are the bookfellers; and it were to be wifhed, that inftead of taking into their pay, for cheapnefs fake, fuperficial, if not paltry hands, they would exert their ability and intereft, for the joint good both of the language and the fciences. They who do, certainly deferve both great praife and encouragement.

What a fair field is here for the real patrons of fciences, to fignalize their patronage!

ARTICLE IV.

Whether it be poffible to invent a learned language, properly fo called.

Some eminent geniufes confidering the faults and defects in all known languages have wifhed that the fciences had a peculiar language, not borrowed from any nation, but the pure invention of philofophers, in a word, *truly learned*; a language, in which each idea fhould have its diftinct type and character, incommunicable to any other ideas, which would, *at once*, put an end to any impropriety, figure and ambiguity. Such a language might confift folely of written characters; or thefe characters might farther be utterable by articulate founds. In the firft cafe it would be like the written language of the Chinefe, which is rather a characteriftic, than a language, and this is an advantage which moft of thofe, who are for the execution of this fcheme, would be contented with. What principally feeds their hopes, is the improvement which

which mathematics have received from the language of algebra: let us, say they, invent an algebra for the other branches of human knowledge, and they will soon come to be equally improved. This project farther offers to them a most delightful prospect: that by means of an universal language, the learned of all nations may easily, and consequently will carry on a literary commerce, and reciprocally communicate their discoveries.

To me, I own, all these hopes appear to stand but on a slender foundation: I have objections and doubts to offer, both against the possibility of such a language, and its supposed utility. These objections I submit to the academy's decision. And first, The instance of algebra weighs little with me. The difference between the other sciences and mathematics, is too wide to expect similar effects. In resolving a geometrical problem, I, in some measure, compose the language which I am to use in the solution; and this small number of characters is the more easily retained, as being of my own choice; for however refractory and stubborn the memory be against admitting the discoveries of another, it is very impressible and retentive, in whatever is of our own invention (*i*).

But in every other scientifical operation, the reasonings are complicated with many foreign ideas, often taken from very different sciences; and this is the case even of mixed geometry itself. To which I add, that a person would not always have the making of his own characteristic; he would be obliged to use that which had been once received into the language of the learned; that is, he would be obliged to learn by heart an infinite number of characters. The reason is self-evident: in elucidating a mathematical subject, I draw before me and my reader what lines are to be denoted by certain characters; or I have other means of knowing

(*i*) A friend of mine has contrived an alphabet, by means of which he can perfectly represent on paper all the imaginable sounds of all languages. So accustomed is he to it, that he cannot be brought to think this alphabet would be very difficult for another to learn. Yet this would certainly be the case with me; at least, in all the languages which I have studied, the alphabet was what always put me to the most trouble, and I am apt to think that, except those whose memory may be accounted a prodigy, it has been so to others.

them,

them, without any poffibility of miftake. On this account it is, that the characters always depend on my choice; whereas, in the fciences, where the meaning of characters cannot be indicated on paper by fenfible images, I muft neceffarily make ufe of figns, already known in fome of the eftablifhed languages; and of which the import is univerfally agreed on, as *marriage, concubinage, polygamy, adultery, fornication, glory, ambition, humility, bafenefs,* &c. All thefe figns might otherwife convey to the reader, ideas quite different from thofe which I intend.

The fame reflection exhibits to us a ftill greater diftance between the algebra of the mathematicians, and the characteriftics of the other fciences. No geometrician can be miftaken in the algebraic character: the lines, however characterifed, are before his eyes, that it is eafy for him to define, and his definitions are infallible.

In other branches of fcience, writers cannot always delineate the images of the objects to which they have annexed certain names; though neither of us be ignorant perfons, both may be miftaken; they in their definitions and I in my application of them: fo that a characteriftic of this kind, will be ever obfcure and uncertain. What I faid above, concerning the definition of marriage *(k)*, may here ferve for an illuftration; and if we fuppofe that the inventor of the characteriftic defines marriage, as fome divines have, A junction of two perfons, of different fexes, with a view to the generation, and bringing up of children, it is very clear, that this word has given him an idea very different from that which it conveys to thofe nations where polygamy obtains. In a word, a fcience, which is the very empire of evidence and certainty, and the demonftrations of which fcarce admit of any foreign objects, by no means warrants a conclufion to more complicated branches of knowledge, and thefe ufually refting only on probabilities.

The inftance of the Chinefe appears to me the ftrongeft argument againft the fcheme of the learned language, or the univerfal characteriftic. I cannot exactly fay of how many thoufands of characters the Chinefe language

(k) Pag: 15, 16.

is at present composed; but prodigious as the number is, it would be still more prodigious, as the sciences improved. How many new characters would botany alone require? All accounts agree, that the literati of China spend life in learning their language, and, after all, die before they have gone through the tedious task. This is laying out life in making an instrument, and then, where is the time for making use of it? The length of time taken up in learning Latin seems to us an age; and the people held out to us for model, bestows the whole course of life in its characteristic. Is it to be wondered at that this nation, otherwise so capable of mental improvements, has, for these two thousand years, since literature obtained among them, made no greater progress; but its *ne plus ultra* seems to be the keeping or preservation of what it indeed acquired very early, but which it cannot encrease? Three hundred years ago, when the Chinese were already a lettered nation, we were barbarians; but how have we outstripped them within that short space? One century has carried us to heights, which they have not been able to reach in twenty. Of this, natural philosophy, astronomy and gunnery, are incontestible proofs; and as to the latter, it is observable, that the Chinese were acquainted with the use of gunpowder long before us. Were we incumbered with so laborious, and so endless a characteristic, our modern *Promethei*, now busied in the investigation of the creator's most abstruse secrets, would still be conning over their alphabet.

But so much for algebra and China: and let us proceed to more direct objections against the learned language.

1. This language, to answer all wants, would require a prodigious quantity of characters, as soon to tire the efforts of the greatest genius; invention would be crushed and stupified by this load on the memory.

Our languages happily keep clear of this enormous fault by giving to one identical word several meanings, which are easily distinguishable by the connection of the discourse, that for an equal number of ideas, we want scarce a tenth part of the characters with which the hypothesis of the learned language is unavoidably clogged.

2. Were

2. Were this language to be sat down in writing, this would still be a much heavier burden on the memory. We have a kind of propensity to associate ideas to sounds, but not at all to figures. The former is natural to man; and if, at our birth, we had not found a language ready prepared for us, we should soon have set about inventing one; whereas writing is a work of art, the invention of which, probably, is by some thousands of years, posterior to the first language.

3. But granting that this language may be spoken, as well as written; its sounds will appear to all nations equally foreign, or, to speak like a Greek, equally barbarous; and foreign sounds are much more difficult to be retained than the national, our ear being used to those, and we are acquainted with their derivations and analogies. Let the difficulty our memory finds in an American proper name, be compared with its readiness in retaining those of our own nation *(l)*.

I should farther apprehend, that the pronunciation of this learned language would not only be extremely difficult, but offensive to the ear. The alterations and contractions to which our common languages are subject have cleared them of that ruggedness, leaving in them such words only as are easily pronounced, and agreeable to the ear. As nature has been filing and polishing them for above these thousand years, they may be looked on as its work; whereas the learned language would be only the production of art, an imitation of nature: and as, if I mistake not, it should be invariable, it would admit of no contractions, and be totally unimpressible by either file or plane.

4. It is not by use, but by an artificial instruction, that we are to learn all these sounds or characters: a fresh torture to memory! We easily become acquainted with a language we are daily speaking, and which is current in common life, especially if we take in some grammatical assistance, yet will this study put us to very tiresome difficulties, when all our help and instruction is to come from art only. What a time is taken

---

(l) See my treatise *on Memory*.

up in learning a little Latin, and how soon do we make a progress in the living languages!

It is certain, that the want of being sufficiently acquainted with the Latin tongue, keeps the mind in a kind of childhood, and depriving it of several discoveries, ever leaves great voids in its knowledge. Yet few of the learned can be said to have any thing of a perfect acquaintance with the Latin: and would not their case be much worse, if, instead of the Latin, they were to study a language much more difficult, and with nothing of its agreeableness? Farther, together with this natural language, there will still be a necessity for learning the Latin, and the other learned languages. The new characteristic would not let us into the discoveries of past times: the sources of ancient history would not be found in it: and lastly, those respectable books from which religion is taken are written in Greek and Hebrew, and not in this characteristic.

5. But granting that all these obstacles may be surmounted, and that men of letters will come into this new language so extremely difficult, nothing but pernicious consequences can result from this use. The body of the people, and all who are not learned by profession, will be daily sinking deeper into ignorance: the characteristic throws up a partition between them and the sciences, as the hieroglyphics among the Egyptians. No middle class is left between the scholar and the rude plebeian.

How very detrimental this would prove to the sciences, has been shewn in all the passages of this dissertation, relating to the benefit accruing to them from the richness of the natural language. But the people would be still much more wretched, were knowledge so far confined to schools, as to be totally out of their reach. Civil life cannot dispense with the want of it. When science takes its flight, a thousand conveniencies and gratifications vanish with it; and especially there is no rank of life but would be deprived of an inexhaustible source of delights, varying as the mind is disposed, and which affords such great relief in those vacant hours which cannot always be filled up by sensual indulgencies. How tiresomely, or rather how scandalously uniform would be the life of an
officer,

officer, in times of peace, without this refource? What has a greater tendency to plunge him into idlenefs, or which is worfe, into licentioufnefs? When I compare the multitude of military gentlemen, void of any tafte for literature, with the officers of the Orleans regiment, garrifoned here in the month of November, 1757, who behaved as if they came only to make ufe of our library, I cannot forbear moft heartily pitying the one, and congratulating the other. Laftly, as the worft confequence of a characteriftic peculiar to the learned, the people would be left to their profound impoftures. This is no more than what happened to the Egyptians in thofe times when all difcoveries were concealed under enigmatical hieroglyphics. Had all the electrical experiments made in our time, been enveloped in the veil of the characteriftic, and known only to the learned, how eafily might they have formed a combination for impofing on credulous minds? and the fecret junto, by falfe miracles, and ingenious preftiges, have fet up a kind of facred tyranny? Opportunity tempts, and the eafinefs of impofing increafes the number of impoftors. The example of ancient nations, I think, might ferve us for a document.

But fhould my fears be thought groundlefs, at leaft, it is indifputably certain, that the characteriftic would extremely impoverifh our mother-tongues, and thus our loffes would over-balance any gains it might bring to us.

Is the wifh of feeing the fciences refcued from their fervitude to the Latin tongue, and to hear them fpeak the living language, well grounded? Whatever can be faid in fupport of this wifh, makes equally ftrong for me.

I have intimated, that the learned language muft be unalterable; and, I imagine, that they who flatter themfelves to find that advantage in it, will be for afking me what equivalent I can contraft with it? But is not this really felf-delufion? I fhould be very apprehenfive, that this language, as to its effential part, I mean the fignification of the characters, would be more variable than any of the living languages. Nothing is more changeable than the technical language of philofophers; or indeed, than technical terms in general. Every reformer of philosophy, every head of a sect, strikes out a new language, and prescribes new definitions, which is no less than changeing the meaning of the established terms. It is natural, that he who imagines he has created ideas unperceived by any before himself, should, in expressing them, make use of words, which before had appeared to him useless and superfluous. Now I say, that in a language, conducted by the learned only, these variations must be both more frequent and more abrupt, than in any other living national language.

These are entirely and absolutely democratical; words cannot be deprived of their received meaning, but by the consent of the people, and the gradual introduction of a contrary custom; whereas an author treats the technical language he makes use of, with all the arbitrariness of despotism. He says, this is the meaning I fix to this term, this is the definition I give of it: we then are all obliged to understand him, as he has declared he will be understood, and as little can we contest that right with him, as prescribe to the algebraist what lines he shall call A and what B. This writer's language, on such an increase of his readers and disciples as to form a numerous party for him, will become the idiom of a sect; and we may take it for granted that this is the case; at least, once in twenty-five years:—in twenty-five years! Has not Germany, since the beginning of this century, already seen three heads of sects? I mean Thomasius, Wolff, and Crusius; and these geniusses of a very different cast? One happy circumstance, however, in all this is, that these new idioms do not change the national language, and that those men of learning, who do not affect singularity, and will not be led like scholars, persevere in a faithful attachment to the ancient language.

What can secure a characteristic, or a language known only to the learned, from such changes? Unless all nations will come into the same sect, and adopt the like variations of the learned language, which is not to be expected. This language will soon split into as many dialects as nations: and the misfortune is, that the meaning of learned languages, when once lost, is much more difficult to recover than to revive the dead language

of

of a whole nation. This is not the place for expatiating on the causes of this phenomenon; experience indeed sufficiently proves it. In explaining antient monuments, is it not in the technical terms of philosophers that the greatest difficulty lies? And books full of these terms, are not they the first in growing obscure? Definitions are but a weak remedy against this obscurity; either being themselves obscure and defective, or the import of the terms of which they are composed, have been likewise lost.

This new language will be no more secure against errors, than our common language: every man of professed learning must be allowed to introduce his notions into this scientific idiom, or he will complain that every thing cannot be expressed in it. Should he entertain chimerical ideas of things not existing, or which being up of contradictions, cannot exist, he will be for realizing those non-entities, by a character of the learned language. The divine, for instance, who believes that God is substantially present every where, and yet holds the same divine substance to be more immediately present to believers, will require a particular character for this impossible omnipresence, his ideas of which are only negative.

Will the learned language be so far indulged, as to characterize the nature of objects, by means of some analogous combination of the signs; as some American languages, for instance, call the lion, *the great and mischievous cat?* Then, as large a field will be thrown open to the man of letters for introducing his false notions into the language, as the people has at present by means of etymologies. Then, may every one, according to his particular way of thinking, coin a new word; and this puts me in mind of the tower of Babel. I see all that confusion breaking in upon us, against which the democratic form of our languages is usually a preventive, by admitting no term till approved of by the people. Or, on the contrary, if every object is to retain its first denomination, who will warrant that denomination to be right? And if any errors had crept into it, still should we be deprived of the resource which our languages afford us in synonimes, these, if I rightly understand the scheme, being excluded from the learned language as superfluities.

The want of synonimes would subject us to another loss. It often happens, that when deceived by the accessory ideas of a word, the synonime undeceives us, or, at least, shews us the object in its true point of light.

Synonimes farther serve to relieve both the ear, which monotony tires, and the mind, the attention of which it blunts. They therefore who imagine that the exclusion of synonimes would embellish a language, seem not over-well acquainted with the organ of hearing, nor the nature of the human heart.

This learned characteristic would be absolutely void of all pathetic terms, and glowing expressions, and likewise of those improper, but most energetic terms, which often, by a bare comparison, throw both light and beauty on the whole of a subject.

This language therefore would be extremely jejune, uniform, and disagreeable; as void of graces or ornaments as the signs of algebra; whereas the beauty of language is of more importance to the sciences than would at first be imagined. Without it, attention soon drops into a languor, against which the love of sciences alone is not able to bear it up, whereas the beauties of language keep it awake. The agreeable ideas, which, as I may say, play before our mind, serve to entertain it amidst the profound meditations with which it is taken up. Farther, the learned language would bring a double labour and trouble on us; the words requiring very nearly as much as things: and, for the reasons alledged in the preceding articles, could never become so easy and familiar to us, as our mother-tongues, nor even as the Latin; that we should find ourselves in the difficult case of one who is to study or teach philosophy in a language with which he has but a very middling acquaintance.

The graces of language elevate genius, whereas it is cramped by jejuneness; and most discoveries are rather the fruits of genius, than the result of forced meditations, or systematical demonstrations. A happy
association

association of ideas lays open inlarged views; and it is not till we have been stricken with them, that we employ ourselves in search of arguments for supporting and realizing them. Thus Archimedes, amidst all his unwearied endeavours, could not solve his own problem; not even when the whole strength of his mind was bent on it. He goes to refresh himself in the bath, and at the very instant of his plunging into the water, the solution rose into his mind of itself. Had he been thinking of it at that juncture, it certainly would have escaped him. It was to his thinking on something else, that he owed the transporting discovery. Genius, what seems a ray from heaven, and which, amidst a thousand paths, all leading to different truths, hits precisely on that, leading to the truth in question. Genius, I say, is rendered more lively and active by pleasure and beauty; whereas it is benumbed by abstractions and profundity. From no other source can be deduced those new thoughts, which the philosophic poet brings forth, as it were fortuitously, in the fits of his enthusiasm, and which, however, stand the most rigid text, and may be accounted oracles.

I can here scarce forbear, vindicating the amenities of stile, from the unjust contempt of that saturnine philosophy, which calls them trash, fit only for the futile tribes of poets and wits; and evincing how much that universal instinct, which forms the language of nations, adapts itself to the wants of human nature, and, in a word, shews how much the variations of sounds, harmony, imagery, and figures, interweaving in the discourse, pleasurable ideas, favour meditation, and elevate the genius. But I am within sight of my conclusion; and this would be launching out into fresh matter, which would carry me little short of that which was the formal subject of the discourse.

A science laid down to us in the language of common life, will be always better learned than when delivered in a technical language, and the best teachers of philosophy, are they who bring all notions to the level of common sense. But it is manifest that this is an advantage quite incompatible with the learned language.

Lastly,

Lastly, I am perſuaded that a characteriſtic of a new invention would, in point of utility, be inferior to the common languages of nations, in a thouſand reſpects, which I cannot previouſly determine. The diſcovery muſt however be undertaken only by one ſingle ſcholar, and, conſequently, his deciſion muſt be abſolute: but whoever this inventive ſcholar be, I ſhall not lay ſuch a ſtreſs on him as on the democracy of a whole nation. The metaphyſics of language is not yet ſufficiently cultivated; and were that as far as poſſible, very few would underſtand it, ſo as to be able to make uſe of it. Beſides an accurate knowledge of man, it ſuppoſes a very extenſive acquaintance both with philoſophy and philology; and theſe are qualities not eaſily found in one perſon; as the academy itſelf has obſerved in the *ſummary of the diſcourſe*, on which it was pleaſed to confer the prize.

INDEX.

www.ingramcontent.com/pod-product-compliance
Lightning Source LLC
Chambersburg PA
CBHW020155170426
43199CB00010B/1048